2025 Roman

Catholic Sunday Missal

Your Guide to Mass Readings, Worship, and the Grace
of the Liturgical Year

Note: Scripture quotations in this work are taken from the Douay-Rheims Bible

Thank You

Dear Beloved Reader,

Thank you for choosing the *2025 Roman Catholic Sunday Missal* as your companion in faith this year. It is an honor and a blessing to journey with you through the sacred rhythms of the liturgical year, connecting you to the living Word of God and the life-giving mystery of the Eucharist.

Your decision to engage with this missal reflects a deep desire to grow closer to Christ and to live out your Catholic faith with greater devotion. I pray this book enriches your spiritual life, strengthens your relationship with God, and deepens your appreciation for the beauty and depth of our Catholic traditions.

This missal is not merely a book—it is a tool for transformation. With each Scripture reading, prayer, and reflection, my hope is that you find inspiration, comfort, and encouragement to live a life centered on Christ.

I am profoundly grateful for your trust in this work and for allowing it to be a part of your spiritual journey. Your support means the world to me and fuels my mission to create resources that nurture faith, inspire prayer, and draw hearts closer to God.

As you use this missal throughout the year, may you find joy in its pages, strength in its guidance, and peace in its prayers. Above all, may it lead you into a deeper encounter with the boundless love of God, who calls each of us to holiness and wholeness. Thank you for your faith, for your prayers, and for being a part of this journey.

With gratitude and blessings,

Esther W. Dawson

Content

Introduction

Welcome to the *2025 Roman Catholic Sunday Missal!* This book is your companion on the journey of faith, offering guidance, inspiration, and prayerful reflection for every Sunday of the year. Rooted in the timeless traditions of the Catholic Church, this missal is designed to enrich your participation in the Holy Mass, deepen your understanding of Scripture, and draw you closer to the heart of God.

The Gift of Sunday

Sunday is far more than the first day of the week; it is the Lord's Day. From the earliest days of Christianity, Sunday has held a unique place in the life of the faithful. It is the day of Christ's Resurrection, the victory of life over death and hope over despair. Each Sunday, we gather as a Church family to celebrate the Eucharist, the source and summit of our faith.

Sunday Mass is a sacred moment when heaven touches earth. Through the Word proclaimed and the Sacrament received, we encounter the living Christ. It is a time to step away from the busyness of life and enter into God's peace. For one hour each week, we are invited to lay our burdens at the altar, offer our praise and thanksgiving, and allow God's grace to renew us.

This weekly celebration is not just a personal moment with God but a communal act of worship. Across the world, Catholics of every nation, language, and culture unite in one faith, one prayer, and one Eucharist. As we gather in our parishes, we are reminded that we are part of something far greater than ourselves—a global Church on a mission to bring the love of Christ to the world.

What This Missal Offers

This missal is much more than a collection of readings and prayers; it is a spiritual guide to help you live the liturgical year with intention and devotion. It is a tool for spiritual growth, offering opportunities to reflect, pray, and act on the Word of God in your daily life.

Every Sunday entry includes:

- **Scripture Readings**: The First Reading, Responsorial Psalm, Second Reading, and Gospel as proclaimed in the Mass, along with the Alleluia verse.

- **Reflections**: Insights into the deeper meaning of the readings, highlighting their connection to our Catholic faith and their relevance to our lives today.

- **A Call to Respond**: Questions and prompts to help you reflect on the Word of God and live it out in concrete ways.

- **Prayer**: A heartfelt prayer inspired by the day's themes to guide your conversations with God.

- **Challenges for the Week**: Practical ways to live out the Gospel message in your everyday interactions and relationships.

- **Space for Notes**: A place to record your thoughts, prayers, and inspirations as you journey through the year.

This structure is intended to make every Sunday a meaningful step in your spiritual journey, equipping you to encounter Christ at Mass and carry His light into the world.

The Beauty of the Liturgical Year

The Catholic liturgical year is a sacred rhythm that immerses us in the life of Christ. From the anticipation of Advent to the joy of Christmas, the penitential journey of Lent to the triumph of Easter, and the steady growth of Ordinary Time, the Church invites us to walk with Jesus through His birth, ministry, passion, death, and resurrection.

Each Sunday is a milestone on this journey. Feast days and solemnities like Epiphany, Pentecost, and Christ the King enrich our worship, drawing us into the mysteries of our faith. Ordinary Sundays offer moments of quiet growth, as we learn from Christ's teachings and reflect on His example.

The liturgical year is also a profound reminder of God's presence in every season of life. Just as the natural world moves through cycles of growth and renewal, so too does our spiritual life. By living the rhythm of the Church year, we align our hearts with God's plan for salvation and open ourselves to His grace.

Encountering God in the Mass

At the heart of every Sunday is the Holy Mass, a sacred encounter with the living God. In the Liturgy of the Word, God speaks to us through Scripture, offering wisdom, comfort, and challenge. In the Liturgy of the Eucharist, we receive the Body and Blood of Christ, the true source of spiritual nourishment and strength.

This missal is designed to help you prepare for and participate in the Mass with greater understanding and devotion. The reflections and prayers in this book will deepen your awareness of God's presence and help you recognize His work in your life.

Mass is not only a celebration of the past—of Christ's life, death, and resurrection—but also a foretaste of the future. It points us toward the heavenly banquet, the eternal joy of being united with God and one another in His kingdom.

A Year of Grace and Growth

The year 2025 is a gift—a new opportunity to grow in faith, hope, and love. Whether you are a lifelong Catholic, a returning member of the Church, or someone seeking a deeper connection with God, this missal is here to accompany you.

As you journey through the pages of this book, may you experience the transforming power of God's Word. Let the reflections inspire you, the prayers comfort you, and the challenges encourage you to live your faith with courage and compassion.

Let's Walk Together

The Church is not just a building or an institution; it is a family of believers walking together toward Christ. As you use this missal, know that you are not alone. Each Sunday, millions of Catholics around the world are praying, reflecting, and celebrating alongside you.

Let this year be a time of renewal and discovery. May the light of Christ guide you, His peace fill your heart, and His love inspire you to share His Gospel with the world.

"Rejoice in the Lord always. I shall say it again: rejoice!" (Philippians 4:4)

Let us begin this journey with open hearts and joyful hope. Together, let us celebrate the gift of Sunday, the beauty of the liturgical year, and the boundless love of God.

January 2025

Sunday, January 5

- Second Sunday of Christmas
- In the United States Epiphany of the Lord – Solemnity

First Reading: Isaiah 60: 1-6

Responsorial Psalm: Psalms 72: 1-2, 7-8, 10-11, 12-13

Second Reading: Ephesians 3: 2-3a, 5-6

Alleluia: Matthew 2: 2

Gospel: Matthew 2: 1-12

Lectionary: 20

The star still shines brightly on this Second Sunday of Christmas, but today it takes on a new dimension. We celebrate the Epiphany, a word meaning "manifestation" or "revelation." The Christ child, once nestled in a manger, now reveals himself to the wider world, represented by the wise men, or magi, who journeyed from afar.

Isaiah Sets the Stage (Isaiah 60: 1-6):

Arise, be enlightened, O Jerusalem: for thy light is come, and the glory of the Lord is risen upon thee.

2 For behold darkness shall cover the earth, and a mist the people: but the Lord shall arise upon thee, and his glory shall be seen upon thee.

3 And the Gentiles shall walk in thy light, and kings in the brightness of thy rising.

4 Lift up thy eyes round about, and see: all these are gathered together, they are come to thee: thy sons shall come from afar, and thy daughters shall rise up at thy side.

5 Then shalt thou see, and abound, and thy heart shall wonder and be enlarged, when the multitude of the sea shall be converted to thee, the. strength of the Gentiles shall come to thee.

6 The multitude of camels shall cover thee, the dromedaries of Madian and Epha: all they from Saba shall come, bringing gold and

frankincense: and shewing forth praise to the Lord.

Our first reading paints a picture of radiant hope. The prophet Isaiah speaks of Jerusalem bathed in dazzling light, a beacon attracting nations from across the globe. This light isn't just physical; it signifies the dawning of a new era, one where God's love and salvation extend far beyond any one people or place.

Responsorial Psalm: Psalms 72: 1-2, 7-8, 10-11, 12-13

R. (11) Lord, every nation on earth will adore you.

1-2 Give to the king thy judgment, O God: and to the king's son thy justice: To judge thy people with justice, and thy poor with judgment.

R. Lord, every nation on earth will adore you.

7 In his days shall justice spring up, and abundance of peace, till the moon be taken sway.

8 And he shall rule from sea to sea, and from the river unto the ends of the earth.

R. Lord, every nation on earth will adore you.

10 The kings of Tharsis and the islands shall offer presents: the kings of the Arabians and of Saba shall bring gifts:

11 And all kings of the earth shall adore him: all nations shall serve him.

R. Lord, every nation on earth will adore you.

12 For he shall deliver the poor from the mighty: and the needy that had no helper.

13 He shall spare the poor and needy: and he shall save the souls of the poor.

R. Lord, every nation on earth will adore you.

A Mystery Revealed (Ephesians 3: 2-3a, 5-6):

2 If yet you have heard of the dispensation of the grace of God which is given me towards you:

3a How that, according to revelation, the mystery has been made known to me.

5 Which in other generations was not known to the sons of men, as it is now revealed to his holy apostles and prophets in the Spirit:

6 That the Gentiles should be fellow heirs, and of the same body, and co-partners of his promise in Christ Jesus, by the gospel:

The passage from Ephesians delves deeper into this mystery. Paul, the apostle, tells us it was once a secret, but now it's been revealed: God's plan for salvation encompasses all humanity, Jew and Gentile alike. We are all invited to become part of God's household, united by our shared faith in Christ.

Alleluia: Matthew 2: 2

R. Alleluia, alleluia.

2 We saw his star at its rising and have come to do him homage.

R. Alleluia, alleluia

The Wise Men Follow the Light (Matthew 2: 1-12):

1 When Jesus therefore was born in Bethlehem of Juda, in the days of king Herod, behold, there came wise men from the east to Jerusalem.

2 Saying, Where is he that is born king of the Jews? For we have seen his star in the east, and are come to adore him.

3 And king Herod hearing this, was troubled, and all Jerusalem with him.

4 And assembling together all the chief priests and the scribes of the people, he inquired of them where Christ should be born.

5 But they said to him: In Bethlehem of Juda. For so it is written by the prophet:

6 And thou Bethlehem the land of Juda art not the least among the princes of Juda: for out of thee shall come forth the captain that shall rule my people Israel.

7 Then Herod, privately calling the wise men, learned diligently of them the time of the star which appeared to them;

8 And sending them into Bethlehem, said: Go and diligently inquire after the child, and when you have found him, bring me word again, that I also may come to adore him.

9 Who having heard the king, went their way; and behold the star which they had seen in the east, went before them, until it came and stood over where the child was.

10 And seeing the star they rejoiced with exceeding great joy.

11 And entering into the house, they found the child with Mary his mother, and falling down they adored him; and opening their treasures, they offered him gifts; gold, frankincense, and myrrh.

12 And having received an answer in sleep that they should not return to Herod, they went back another way into their country.

The Gospel of Matthew brings the story to life with the captivating narrative of the magi. Guided by a star, they embark on a long and arduous journey, driven by a yearning for truth and a desire to witness the newborn king. Their journey is a powerful symbol of our own spiritual quests, the lengths we're willing to go to in search of meaning and connection with the divine.

Reflect & Respond:

- Imagine yourself as one of the magi. What motivates you to undertake this long journey?

- Think about the lights in your own life - the people, places, or experiences that illuminate your path. How can you share that light with others?

- The magi brought gifts of gold, frankincense, and myrrh. What gift would you offer the Christ child?

Prayer:

Dear God, Thank you for revealing your love to the world through the birth of your Son, Jesus Christ. Open our hearts to the light of your truth, and guide us to share it with others. May we, like the magi, be seekers of truth and instruments of your peace. Amen.

Challenge:

This week, find an opportunity to share the light of Christ's love with someone outside your usual circle.

It could be a kind word, a helping hand, or simply a listening ear.

Notes:_____

_____

_____

_____

_____

_____

_____

_____

_____

_____

_____

_____

_____

_____

_____

_____

_____

_____

_____

_____

_____

_____

_____

_____

_____

_____

_____

_____

_____

_____

_____

_____

_____

_____

Sunday, January 12

- Baptism of the Lord - Feast

First Reading: Isaiah 42: 1-4, 6-7 or Isaiah 40: 1-5, 9-11

Responsorial Psalm: Psalms 104: 1b-2, 3-4, 24-25, 27-28, 29-30

Second Reading: Titus 2: 11-14; 3: 4-7

Alleluia: Luke 3: 16

Gospel: Luke 3: 15-16, 21-22

Lectionary: 21

Today, we revisit the momentous event of Jesus' baptism in the Jordan River, marking the Feast of the Baptism of the Lord. This occasion signifies not just a cleansing ritual, but the official beginning of Jesus' public ministry.

Isaiah Sets the Stage (Isaiah 42: 1-4, 6-7 or Isaiah 40: 1-5, 9-11):

1 Behold my servant, I will uphold him: my elect, my soul delighteth in him: I have given my spirit upon him, he shall bring forth judgment to the Gentiles.

2 He shall not cry, nor have respect to person, neither shall his voice be heard abroad.

3 The bruised reed he shall not break, and smoking flax he shall not quench: he shall bring forth judgment unto truth.

4 He shall not be sad, nor troublesome, till he set judgment in the earth: and the islands shall wait for his law.

6 I the Lord have called thee in justice, and taken thee by the hand, and preserved thee. And I have given thee for a covenant of the people, for a light of the Gentiles:

7 That thou mightest open the eyes of the blind, and bring forth the prisoner out of prison, and them that sit in darkness out of the prison house.

Or

1 Be comforted, be comforted, my people, saith your God.

2 Speak ye to the heart of Jerusalem, and call to her: for her evil is come to an end, her iniquity is forgiven: she hath received of the hand of the Lord double for all her sins.

3 The voice of one crying in the desert: Prepare ye the way of the Lord, make straight in the wilderness the paths of our God.

4 Every valley shall be exalted, and every mountain and hill shall be made low, and the crooked shall become straight, and the rough ways plain.

5 And the glory of the Lord shall be revealed, and all flesh together shall see, that the mouth of the Lord hath spoken.

9 Get thee up upon a high mountain, thou that bringest good tidings to Sion: lift up thy voice with strength, thou that bringest good tidings to Jerusalem: lift it up, fear not. Say to the cities of Juda: Behold your God:

10 Behold the Lord God shall come with strength, and his arm shall rule:

Behold his reward is with him and his work is before him.

11 He shall feed his flock like a shepherd: he shall gather together the lambs with his arm, and shall take them up in his bosom, and he himself shall carry them that are with young.

The prophet Isaiah's words in the first reading provide a powerful backdrop. He speaks of a chosen servant, a light to the nations, who will bring justice and salvation to the world. This servant embodies the qualities Jesus will demonstrate throughout his ministry: compassion, justice, and unwavering commitment to God's will.

Responsorial Psalm: Psalms 104: 1b-2, 3-4, 24-25, 27-28, 29-30

R. (1) O bless the Lord, my soul.

1b O Lord my God, thou art exceedingly great. Thou hast put on praise and beauty:

2 And art clothed with light as with a garment. Who stretchest out the heaven like a pavilion:

R. O bless the Lord, my soul.

3 Who coverest the higher rooms thereof with water. Who makest the clouds thy chariot: who walkest upon the wings of the winds.

4 Who makest thy angels spirits: and thy ministers a burning fire.

R. O bless the Lord, my soul.

24 How great are thy works, O Lord? thou hast made all things in wisdom: the earth is filled with thy riches.

25 So is this great sea, which stretcheth wide its arms: there are creeping things without number: Creatures little and great.

R. O bless the Lord, my soul.

27 All expect of thee that thou give them food in season.

28 What thou givest to them they shall gather up: when thou openest thy hand, they shall all be filled with good.

R. O bless the Lord, my soul.

29 But if thou turnest away thy face, they shall be troubled: thou shalt take away their breath, and they shall fail, and shall return to their dust.

30 Thou shalt send forth thy spirit, and they shall be created: and thou shalt renew the face of the earth.

R. O bless the Lord, my soul.

Titus Calls Us to Live the Light (Titus 2: 11-14; 3: 4-7):

11 For the grace of God our Saviour hath appeared to all men;

12 Instructing us, that, denying ungodliness and worldly desires, we should live soberly, and justly, and godly in this world,

13 Looking for the blessed hope and coming of the glory of the great God and our Saviour Jesus Christ,

14 Who gave himself for us, that he might redeem us from all iniquity, and might cleanse to himself a people acceptable, a pursuer of good works.

3:4 But when the goodness and kindness of God our Saviour appeared:

5 Not by the works of justice, which we have done, but according to his mercy, he saved us, by the laver of regeneration, and renovation of the Holy Ghost;

6 Whom he hath poured forth upon us abundantly, through Jesus Christ our Saviour:

7 That, being justified by his grace, we may be heirs, according to hope of life everlasting.

The passage from Titus offers a message of hope and transformation. The grace of God has appeared, offering us the opportunity to reject ungodliness and live lives marked by self-control, righteousness, and devotion to God. We are called to be reflections of God's light in the world, living with kindness and anticipation of the blessed hope – the glorious appearing of our great God and Savior, Jesus Christ.

Alleluia: Luke 3: 16

R. Alleluia, alleluia.

16 John said: One mightier than I is coming; he will baptize you with the Holy Spirit and with fire.

R. Alleluia, alleluia.

Witnessing the Revelation (Luke 3: 15-16, 21-22):

And as the people were of opinion, and all were thinking in their hearts of John, that perhaps he might be the Christ;

16 John answered, saying unto all: I indeed baptize you with water; but there shall come one mightier than I, the latchet of whose shoes I am not worthy to loose: he shall baptize you with the Holy Ghost, and with fire:

21 Now it came to pass, when all the people were baptized, that Jesus also being baptized and praying, heaven was opened;

22 And the Holy Ghost descended in a bodily shape, as a dove upon him; and a voice came from heaven: Thou art my beloved Son; in thee I am well pleased.

The Gospel of Luke recounts the baptism itself. As Jesus emerges from the water, the heavens open, and the Holy Spirit descends in the form of a dove. A voice booms from heaven, proclaiming Jesus as God's "beloved Son," in whom he is well pleased. This is a pivotal moment, not just for Jesus, but for all humanity. It signifies God's presence actively working in the world through his Son.

Reflect & Respond:

- How does the image of Jesus being baptized challenge our understanding of what it means to be the Son of God?

- The passage from Titus speaks of rejecting ungodliness and living righteously. What are some ways we can strive to live according to these principles?

- Consider the concept of being a "light to the nations." How can you share the light of Christ's love with those around you?

Prayer:

Dear Heavenly Father, thank you for revealing yourself to us through the baptism of your Son. Grant us the wisdom to recognize your presence in our lives and the courage to follow your call. May we be instruments of your love and light in the world. Amen.

Challenge:

This week, take some time to reflect on your own baptism (or a significant spiritual experience in your life). How has it shaped your faith journey? Consider how you can more actively share the light of Christ with the world through your actions and words.

Notes:_____

_____

Sunday,
January 19

- Second Sunday
  in Ordinary Time

First Reading: Isaiah 62: 1-5

Responsorial Psalm: Psalms
96: 1-2a, 2b-3, 7-8, 9-10

Second Reading: First
Corinthians 12: 4-11

Alleluia: Second Thessalonians
2: 14

Gospel: John 2: 1-11

Lectionary: 66

Welcome to the Second Sunday in Ordinary Time! As the Christmas season fades, the focus shifts to the ongoing ministry of Jesus and the lessons he offers us.

Today's readings illuminate themes of inner light, the power of community, and the miraculous potential within each of us.

Isaiah's Vision of Radiant Hope (Isaiah 62: 1-5):

1 For Sion's sake I will not hold my peace, and for the sake of Jerusalem, I will not rest till her just one come forth as brightness, and her saviour be lighted as a lamp.

2 And the Gentiles shall see thy just one, and all kings thy glorious one: and thou shalt be called by a new name, which the mouth of the Lord shall name.

3 And thou shalt be a crown of glory in the hand of the Lord, and a royal diadem in the hand of thy God.

4 Thou shalt no more be called Forsaken: and thy land shall no more be called Desolate: but thou shalt be called My pleasure in her, and thy land inhabited. Because the Lord hath been well pleased with thee: and thy land shall be inhabited.

5 For the young man shall dwell with the virgin, and thy children shall dwell in thee. And the bridegroom shall rejoice over the bride, and thy God shall rejoice over thee.

The prophet Isaiah paints a captivating picture in the first reading. He speaks of Jerusalem bathed in radiant light, a beacon of hope for all nations. This light isn't just a physical phenomenon; it signifies God's unwavering love and purpose for his people. God promises to never again hide his face from Jerusalem, symbolizing his enduring presence and protection.

Responsorial Psalm: Psalms 96: 1-2a, 2b-3, 7-8, 9-10

R. (3) Proclaim his marvelous deeds to all the nations.

1 Sing ye to the Lord a new canticle: sing to the Lord, all the earth.

2a Sing ye to the Lord and bless his name.

R. Proclaim his marvelous deeds to all the nations.

2b Shew forth his salvation from day to day.

3 Declare his glory among the Gentiles: his wonders among all people.

R. Proclaim his marvelous deeds to all the nations.

7 Bring ye to the Lord, O ye kindreds of the Gentiles, bring ye to the Lord glory and honour:

8 Bring to the Lord glory unto his name. Bring up sacrifices, and come into his courts:

R. Proclaim his marvelous deeds to all the nations.

9 Adore ye the Lord in his holy court. Let all the earth be moved at his presence.

10 Say ye among the Gentiles, the Lord hath reigned. For he hath corrected the world, which shall not be moved: he will judge the people with justice.

R. Proclaim his marvelous deeds to all the nations.

Unity in Diversity (1 Corinthians 12: 4-11):

4 Now there are diversities of graces, but the same Spirit;

5 And there are diversities of ministries, but the same Lord;

6 And there are diversities of operations, but the same God, who worketh all in all.q

7 And the manifestation of the Spirit is given to every man unto profit.

8 To one indeed, by the Spirit, is given the word of wisdom: and to another, the word of knowledge, according to the same Spirit;

9 To another, faith in the same spirit; to another, the grace of healing in one Spirit;

10 To another, the working of miracles; to another, prophecy; to another, the discerning of spirits; to another, diverse kinds of tongues; to another, interpretation of speeches.

11 But all these things one and the same Spirit worketh, dividing to every one according as he will.

The passage from 1 Corinthians beautifully captures the essence of Christian community. Paul emphasizes that the Holy Spirit bestows a variety of gifts on each believer, creating a rich tapestry of talents and contributions. Just as the body is comprised of many parts, each with its unique function, the Church thrives when its members work together in unity, utilizing their diverse gifts for the common good.

Alleluia: Second Thessalonians 2: 14

R. Alleluia, alleluia.

14 God has called us through the Gospel to possess the glory of our Lord Jesus Christ.

R. Alleluia, alleluia.

The Miracle at Cana (John 2: 1-11):

1 And the third day, there was a marriage in Cana of Galilee: and the mother of Jesus was there.

2 And Jesus also was invited, and his disciples, to the marriage.

3 And the wine failing, the mother of Jesus saith to him: They have no wine.

4 And Jesus saith to her: Woman, what is that to me and to thee? my hour is not yet come.

5 His mother saith to the waiters: Whatsoever he shall say to you, do ye.

6 Now there were set there six waterpots of stone, according to the manner of the purifying of the Jews, containing two or three measures apiece.

7 Jesus saith to them: Fill the waterpots with water. And they filled them up to the brim.

8 And Jesus saith to them: Draw out now, and carry to the chief steward of the feast. And they carried it.

9 And when the chief steward had tasted the water made wine, and knew not whence it was, but the waiters knew who had drawn the water; the chief steward calleth the bridegroom,

10 And saith to him: Every man at first setteth forth good wine, and when men have well drunk, then that which is worse. But thou hast kept the good wine until now.

11 This beginning of miracles did Jesus in Cana of Galilee; and manifested his glory, and his disciples believed in him.

The Gospel of John introduces us to a pivotal moment in Jesus' ministry - the miracle at Cana.

At a wedding celebration, Jesus transforms water into wine, demonstrating his power and compassion. This act not only saves the wedding feast from embarrassment but also foreshadows his ability to transform our lives and bring joy where there may be lack.

Reflect & Respond:

- How does Isaiah's vision of radiant light resonate with your own understanding of God's presence?

- Consider the concept of spiritual gifts in 1 Corinthians. What unique talents or abilities do you bring to your community?

- The miracle at Cana highlights Jesus' power to transform. Is there an area of your life where you seek transformation or a miracle?

Prayer:

Almighty God, thank you for the gift of your Holy Spirit, who equips us with unique gifts to serve your Church. Open our hearts to recognize the light within ourselves and the light you bring to the world through others. May we work together in unity, sharing your love and transforming lives according to your will. Amen.

Challenge:

This week, take some time to identify your own spiritual gifts and how you can use them to contribute to your community. Perhaps you have a talent for music, organization, or simply offering a listening ear. Reach out to someone in need and share your light.

Notes:_____

_____

_____

_____

_____

Sunday, January 26

- Third Sunday in Ordinary Time

First Reading: Nehemiah 8: 2-4a, 5-6, 8-10

Responsorial Psalm: Psalms 19: 8, 9, 10, 15

Second Reading: First Corinthians 12: 12-30 or First Corinthians 12: 12-14, 27

Alleluia: Luke 4: 18

Gospel: Luke 1: 1-4; 4: 14-21

Lectionary: 69

This Third Sunday in Ordinary Time offers a powerful message about the importance of community, the fulfillment of prophecy, and the seeds of promise that lie within each of us.

Nehemiah Rebuilds Hope (Nehemiah 8: 2-4a, 5-6, 8-10):

2 Then Esdras the priest brought the law before the multitude of men and women, and all those that could understand, in the first day of the seventh month.

3 And he read it plainly in the street that was before the water gate, from the morning until midday, before the men, and the women, and all those that could understand: and the ears of all the people were attentive to the book.

4a And Esdras the scribe stood upon a step of wood, which he had made to speak upon.

5 And Esdras opened the book before all the people: for he was above all the people: and when he had opened it, all the people stood.

6 And Esdras blessed the Lord the great God: and all the people answered, Amen, amen: lifting up their hands: and they bowed down, and adored God with their faces to the ground.

8 And they read in the book of the law of God distinctly and plainly to

be understood: and they understood when it was read.

9 And Nehemias (he is Athersatha) and Esdras the priest and scribe, and the Levites who interpreted to all the people, said: This is a holy day to the Lord our God: do not mourn, nor weep: for all the people wept, when they heard the words of the law.

10 And he said to them: Go, eat fat meats, and drink sweet wine, and send portions to them that have not prepared for themselves: because it is the holy day of the Lord, and be not sad: for the joy of the Lord is our strength.

The first reading takes us back to the time of Nehemiah, a leader who returned to Jerusalem after exile to rebuild the city walls. He gathers the people to hear the reading of the Law, a reminder of their faith and God's enduring promises. The people respond with weeping and joy, overwhelmed by the beauty and power of the word. This passage highlights the importance of community in fostering faith and the transformative power of scripture.

Responsorial Psalm: Psalms 19: 8, 9, 10, 15

R. (John 6:63c) Your words, Lord, are Spirit and life.

8 The law of the Lord is unspotted, converting souls: the testimony of the Lord is faithful, giving wisdom to little ones.

R. Your words, Lord, are Spirit and life.

9 The justices of the Lord are right, rejoicing hearts: the commandment of the Lord is lightsome, enlightening the eyes.

R. Your words, Lord, are Spirit and life.

10 The fear of the Lord is holy, enduring for ever and ever: the judgments of the Lord are true, justified in themselves.

R. Your words, Lord, are Spirit and life.

15 And the words of my mouth shall be such as may please: and the meditation of my heart always in thy sight. O Lord, my helper, and my redeemer.

R. Your words, Lord, are Spirit and life.

Unity in the Body of Christ (1 Corinthians 12: 12-30 or 12: 12-14, 27):

12 For as the body is one, and hath many members; and all the members of the body, whereas they are many, yet are one body, so also is Christ.

13 For in one Spirit were we all baptized into one body, whether Jews or Gentiles, whether bond or free; and in one Spirit we have all been made to drink.

14 For the body also is not one member, but many.

15 If the foot should say, because I am not the hand, I am not of the body; is it therefore not of the body?

16 And if the ear should say, because I am not the eye, I am not of the body; is it therefore not of the body?

17 If the whole body were the eye, where would be the hearing? If the whole were hearing, where would be the smelling?

18 But now God hath set the members every one of them in the body as it hath pleased him.

19 And if they all were one member, where would be the body?

20 But now there are many members indeed, yet one body.

21 And the eye cannot say to the hand: I need not thy help; nor again the head to the feet: I have no need of you.

22 Yea, much more those that seem to be the more feeble members of the body, are more necessary.

23 And such as we think to be the less honourable members of the body, about these we put more abundant honour; and those that are our uncomely parts, have more abundant comeliness.

24 But our comely parts have no need: but God hath tempered the body together, giving to that which wanted the more abundant honour,

25 That there might be no schism in the body; but the members might be mutually careful one for another.

26 And if one member suffer any thing, all the members suffer with

it; or if one member glory, all the members rejoice with it.

27 Now you are the body of Christ, and members of member.

28 And God indeed hath set some in the church; first apostles, secondly prophets, thirdly doctors; after that miracles; then the graces of healing, helps, governments, kinds of tongues, interpretations of speeches.

29 Are all apostles? Are all prophets? Are all doctors?

30 Are all workers of miracles? Have all the grace of healing? Do all speak with tongues? Do all interpret?

Or

12 For as the body is one, and hath many members; and all the members of the body, whereas they are many, yet are one body, so also is Christ.

13 For in one Spirit were we all baptized into one body, whether Jews or Gentiles, whether bond or free; and in one Spirit we have all been made to drink.

14 For the body also is not one member, but many.

27 Now you are the body of Christ, and members of member.

The alternate selections from 1 Corinthians offer a continuation of the theme of community from last week. Paul emphasizes that just as the human body is comprised of many parts, each with its own function, the Church thrives on the diversity of its members. The Holy Spirit bestows unique gifts on each believer, creating a harmonious whole where everyone contributes according to their strengths. This passage reminds us that we are stronger together, united in our purpose to serve God.

Alleluia: Luke 4: 18

R. Alleluia, alleluia.

18 The Lord sent me to bring glad tidings to the poor, and to proclaim liberty to captives.

R. Alleluia, alleluia.

The Word Made Flesh (Luke 1: 1-4; 4: 14-21):

1 Forasmuch as many have taken in hand to set forth in order a

narration of the things that have been accomplished among us;

2 According as they have delivered them unto us, who from the beginning were eyewitnesses and ministers of the word:

3 It seemed good to me also, having diligently attained to all things from the beginning, to write to thee in order, most excellent Theophilus,

4 That thou mayest know the verity of those words in which thou hast been instructed.

4:14 And Jesus returned in the power of the spirit, into Galilee, and the fame of him went out through the whole country.

15 And he taught in their synagogues, and was magnified by all.

16 And he came to Nazareth, where he was brought up: and he went into the synagogue, according to his custom, on the sabbath day; and he rose up to read.

17 And the book of Isaias the prophet was delivered unto him. And as he unfolded the book, he found the place where it was written:

18 The Spirit of the Lord is upon me. Wherefore he hath anointed me to preach the gospel to the poor, he hath sent me to heal the contrite of heart,

19 To preach deliverance to the captives, and sight to the blind, to set at liberty them that are bruised, to preach the acceptable year of the Lord, and the day of reward.

20 And when he had folded the book, he restored it to the minister, and sat down. And the eyes of all in the synagogue were fixed on him.

21 And he began to say to them: This day is fulfilled this scripture in your ears.

The Gospel of Luke presents a beautiful tapestry of prophecy and fulfillment. The first part introduces the author, Luke, who meticulously researched the life of Jesus. The second part takes us to the beginning of Jesus' public ministry. He returns to Galilee, empowered by the Holy Spirit, and his message of hope and liberation resonates throughout the region. Jesus fulfills the prophecy of Isaiah, proclaiming good news to the poor, release to the captives, and sight to the blind.

Reflect & Respond:

- How does the story of Nehemiah rebuilding Jerusalem inspire you to build something positive in your own community?

- Consider the concept of the Church as the Body of Christ in 1 Corinthians. What role do you play in this body?

- Jesus' message in Luke focuses on bringing good news and liberation. Who in your life needs to hear a message of hope or experience some form of liberation?

Prayer:

Dear God, we thank you for the gift of your word and the community of faith that sustains us. Help us to be active participants in your Church, using our unique gifts to build each other up and share your love with the world. May we be instruments of hope and liberation, following the example of your Son, Jesus Christ. Amen.

Challenge:

This week, find an opportunity to connect with your faith community or a group that shares your values. Offer your time, talents, or simply a listening ear. Remember, even small acts of service can have a ripple effect, creating a more connected and compassionate world.

Notes:_____

_____

_____

_____

_____

_____

_____

_____

_____

February2025

Sunday, February 2

- Presentation of the Lord - Feast

First Reading: Malachi 3: 1-4

Responsorial Psalm: Psalms 24: 7, 8, 9, 10

Second Reading: Hebrews 2: 14-18

Alleluia: Luke 2: 32

Gospel: Luke 2: 22-40 or Luke 2: 22-32

Lectionary: 524

Today, we celebrate the Presentation of the Lord, a feast commemorating the day Mary and Joseph brought Jesus to the temple in Jerusalem, forty days after his birth. This seemingly ordinary act carries profound meaning, highlighting Jesus' identity as the promised Messiah and the light destined to illuminate the world.

Malachi Foretells the Coming Messenger (Malachi 3: 1-4):

1 Behold I send my angel, and he shall prepare the way before my face. And presently the Lord, whom you seek, and the angel of the testament, whom you desire, shall come to his temple. Behold he cometh, saith the Lord of hosts.

2 And who shall be able to think of the day of his coming? and who shall stand to see him? for he is like a refining fire, and like the fuller's herb:

3 And he shall sit refining and cleansing the silver, and he shall purify the sons of Levi, and shall refine them as gold, and as silver, and they shall offer sacrifices to the Lord in justice.

4 And the sacrifice of Juda and of Jerusalem shall please the Lord, as in the days of old, and in the ancient years.

37

The first reading from Malachi sets the stage with a powerful prophecy. The Lord speaks of sending a messenger to prepare the way for his coming. This messenger will refine and purify, ensuring the offerings presented to God are worthy. Malachi's words foreshadow the arrival of John the Baptist, who will pave the way for Jesus' ministry.

Responsorial Psalm: Psalms 24: 7, 8, 9, 10

R. (8) Who is this king of glory? It is the Lord!

7 Lift up your gates, O ye princes, and be ye lifted up, O eternal gates: and the King of Glory shall enter in.

R. Who is this king of glory? It is the Lord!

8 Who is this King of Glory? the Lord who is strong and mighty: the Lord mighty in battle.

R. Who is this king of glory? It is the Lord!

9 Lift up your gates, O ye princes, and be ye lifted up, O eternal gates: and the King of Glory shall enter in.

R. Who is this king of glory? It is the Lord!

10 Who is this King of Glory? the Lord of hosts, he is the King of Glory.

R. Who is this king of glory? It is the Lord!

Sharing in Our Humanity (Hebrews 2: 14-18):

14 Therefore because the children are partakers of flesh and blood, he also himself in like manner hath been partaker of the same: that, through death, he might destroy him who had the empire of death, that is to say, the devil:

15 And might deliver them, who through the fear of death were all their lifetime subject to servitude.

16 For no where doth he take hold of the angels: but of the seed of Abraham he taketh hold.

17 Wherefore it behoved him in all things to be made like unto his brethren, that he might become a

merciful and faithful priest before God, that he might be a propitiation for the sins of the people.

18 For in that, wherein he himself hath suffered and been tempted, he is able to succour them also that are tempted.

The passage from Hebrews delves deeper into Jesus' role as the Messiah. The author emphasizes that Jesus, fully human and fully divine, shared in our human experience. He was tempted in all things yet remained without sin. This shared humanity allows Jesus to empathize with our struggles and act as our compassionate high priest, interceding for us before God.

Alleluia: Luke 2: 32

R. Alleluia, alleluia.

32 A light of revelation to the Gentiles, and glory for your people Israel.

R. Alleluia, alleluia.

A Light for All Nations (Luke 2: 22-40 or Luke 2: 22-32):

22 And after the days of her purification, according to the law of Moses, were accomplished, they carried him to Jerusalem, to present him to the Lord:

23 As it is written in the law of the Lord: Every male opening the womb shall be called holy to the Lord:

24 And to offer a sacrifice, according as it is written in the law of the Lord, a pair of turtledoves, or two young pigeons:

25 And behold there was a man in Jerusalem named Simeon, and this man was just and devout, waiting for the consolation of Israel; and the Holy Ghost was in him.

26 And he had received an answer from the Holy Ghost, that he should not see death, before he had seen the Christ of the Lord.

27 And he came by the Spirit into the temple. And when his parents brought in the child Jesus, to do for him according to the custom of the law,

28 He also took him into his arms, and blessed God, and said:

29 Now thou dost dismiss thy servant, O Lord, according to thy word in peace;

30 Because my eyes have seen thy salvation,

31 Which thou hast prepared before the face of all peoples:

32 A light to the revelation of the Gentiles, and the glory of thy people Israel.

33 And his father and mother were wondering at those things which were spoken concerning him.

34 And Simeon blessed them, and said to Mary his mother: Behold this child is set for the fall, and for the resurrection of many in Israel, and for a sign which shall be contradicted;

35 And thy own soul a sword shall pierce, that, out of many hearts, thoughts may be revealed.

36 And there was one Anna, a prophetess, the daughter of Phanuel, of the tribe of Aser; she was far advanced in years, and had lived with her husband seven years from her virginity.

37 And she was a widow until fourscore and four years; who departed not from the temple, by fastings and prayers serving night and day.

38 Now she, at the same hour, coming in, confessed to the Lord; and spoke of him to all that looked for the redemption of Israel.

39 And after they had performed all things according to the law of the Lord, they returned into Galilee, to their city Nazareth.

40 And the child grew, and waxed strong, full of wisdom; and the grace of God was in him.

Or

22 And after the days of her purification, according to the law of Moses, were accomplished, they carried him to Jerusalem, to present him to the Lord:

23 As it is written in the law of the Lord: Every male opening the womb shall be called holy to the Lord:

24 And to offer a sacrifice, according as it is written in the law of the Lord, a pair of turtledoves, or two young pigeons:

25 And behold there was a man in Jerusalem named Simeon, and this man was just and devout, waiting for the consolation of Israel; and the Holy Ghost was in him.

26 And he had received an answer from the Holy Ghost, that he should not see death, before he had seen the Christ of the Lord.

27 And he came by the Spirit into the temple. And when his parents brought in the child Jesus, to do for him according to the custom of the law,

28 He also took him into his arms, and blessed God, and said:

29 Now thou dost dismiss thy servant, O Lord, according to thy word in peace;

30 Because my eyes have seen thy salvation,

31 Which thou hast prepared before the face of all peoples:

32 A light to the revelation of the Gentiles, and the glory of thy people Israel.

The Gospel of Luke recounts the presentation of Jesus in the temple. Mary and Joseph fulfill the requirements of the Law, offering a sacrifice and dedicating their firstborn son to God. Simeon, a righteous and devout man, is led by the Spirit to the temple. He recognizes Jesus as the Messiah, a light for revelation to the Gentiles and for glory to Israel. This encounter signifies that Jesus' ministry extends beyond the Jewish people, encompassing all nations.

Reflect & Respond:

- How does the prophecy in Malachi resonate with your own understanding of the coming of the Messiah?

- The passage from Hebrews highlights Jesus' shared humanity. In what ways can you connect with Jesus' human experience?

- Simeon recognizes Jesus as a light for all nations. How can you share the light of Christ's love with those from different backgrounds or cultures?

Prayer:

Almighty God, thank you for sending your Son, Jesus Christ, as a light for the world. May we follow his example of humility and obedience. Help us to see the reflection of your divine love in all people, and guide us to share your light with joy and compassion. Amen.

Challenge:

This week, make a conscious effort to reach out to someone from a different background or culture. It could be a simple conversation, a shared meal, or an act of kindness. Remember, even small gestures can bridge divides and foster understanding.

Notes:_____

_____

_____

_____

_____

_____

Sunday, February 9

- Fifth Sunday in Ordinary Time

First Reading: Isaiah 6: 1-2a, 3-8

Responsorial Psalm: Psalms 138: 1-2ab, 2cd-3, 4-5, 7c-8

Second Reading: First Corinthians 15: 1-11 or First Corinthians 15: 3-8, 11

Alleluia: Matthew 4: 19

Gospel: Luke 5: 1-11

Lectionary: 75

This Fifth Sunday in Ordinary Time compels us to contemplate the call of God, the power of faith, and the miraculous potential that unfolds when we step outside our comfort zones.

Isaiah's Vision of God's Glory (Isaiah 6: 1-2a, 3-8):

1 In the year that king Ozias died, I saw the Lord sitting upon a throne high and elevated: and his train filled the temple.

2a Upon it stood the seraphims.

3 And they cried one to another, and said: Holy, holy, holy, the Lord God of hosts, all the earth is full of his glory.

4 And the lintels of the doors were moved at the voice of him that cried, and the house was filled with smoke.

5 And I said: Woe is me, because I have held my peace; because I am a man of unclean lips, and I dwell in the midst of a people that hath unclean lips, and I have seen with my eyes the King the Lord of hosts.

6 And one of the seraphims flew to me, and in his hand was a live coal, which he had taken with the tongs off the altar.

7 And he touched my mouth, and said: Behold this hath touched thy lips, and thy iniquities shall be taken away, and thy sin shall be cleansed.

8 And I heard the voice of the Lord, saying: Whom shall I send? and who shall go for us? And I said: Lo, here am I, send me.

The prophet Isaiah opens the service with a awe-inspiring vision. He witnesses the majesty of God enthroned in the temple, surrounded by heavenly beings proclaiming his holiness. Overcome with a sense of his own unworthiness, Isaiah hears God's voice calling him to be a messenger, to speak God's word even when the message is difficult.

This encounter highlights the transformative power of encountering God's presence and the courage required to answer his call.

Responsorial Psalm: Psalms 138: 1-2ab, 2cd-3, 4-5, 7c-8

R. (1c) In the sight of the angels I will sing your praises, Lord.

1 I will praise thee, O lord, with my whole heart: for thou hast heard the words of my mouth. I will sing praise to thee in the sight of his angels:

2ab I will worship towards thy holy temple, and I will give glory to thy name.

R. In the sight of the angels I will sing your praises, Lord.

2cd For thy mercy, and for thy truth: for thou hast magnified thy holy name above all.

3 In what day soever I shall call upon thee, hear me: thou shall multiply strength in my soul.

R. In the sight of the angels I will sing your praises, Lord.

4 May all the kings of the earth give glory to thee: for they have heard all the words of thy mouth.

5 And let them sing in the ways of the Lord: for great is the glory of the Lord.

R. In the sight of the angels I will sing your praises, Lord.

7c Your right hand hath saved me.

8 The Lord will repay for me: thy mercy, O Lord, endureth for ever: O despise not the work of thy hands.

R. In the sight of the angels I will sing your praises, Lord.

The Gospel of Faith (1 Corinthians 15: 1-11 or 15: 3-8, 11):

1 Now I make known unto you, brethren, the gospel which I preached to you, which also you have received, and wherein you stand;

2 By which also you are saved, if you hold fast after what manner I preached unto you, unless you have believed in vain.

3 For I delivered unto you first of all, which I also received: how that Christ died for our sins, according to the scriptures:

4 And that he was buried, and that he rose again the third day, according to the scriptures:

5 And that he was seen by Cephas; and after that by the eleven.

6 Then he was seen by more than five hundred brethren at once: of whom many remain until this present, and some are fallen asleep.

7 After that, he was seen by James, then by all the apostles.

8 And last of all, he was seen also by me, as by one born out of due time.

9 For I am the least of the apostles, who am not worthy to be called an apostle, because I persecuted the church of God.

10 But by the grace of God, I am what I am; and his grace in me hath not been void, but I have laboured more abundantly than all they: yet not I, but the grace of God with me.

11 For whether I, or they, so we preach, and so you have believed.

Or

3 For I delivered unto you first of all, which I also received: how that Christ died for our sins, according to the scriptures:

4 And that he was buried, and that he rose again the third day, according to the scriptures:

5 And that he was seen by Cephas; and after that by the eleven.

6 Then he was seen by more than five hundred brethren at once: of whom many remain until this present, and some are fallen asleep.

7 After that, he was seen by James, then by all the apostles.

8 And last of all, he was seen also by me, as by one born out of due time.

11 For whether I, or they, so we preach, and so you have believed.

The selected passages from 1 Corinthians focus on the importance of faith, particularly regarding the resurrection of Jesus Christ. Paul, the apostle, reminds the Corinthians of the core tenets of their faith: that Christ died for our sins, was buried, and rose again on the third day. This core belief is the foundation of Christianity and offers hope for eternal life.

Alleluia: Matthew 4: 19

R. Alleluia, alleluia.

19 Come after me and I will make you fishers of men.

R. Alleluia, alleluia.

The Miraculous Catch (Luke 5: 1-11):

1 And it came to pass, that when the multitudes pressed upon him to hear the word of God, he stood by the lake of Genesareth,

2 And saw two ships standing by the lake: but the fishermen were gone out of them, and were washing their nets.

3 And going into one of the ships that was Simon's, he desired him to draw back a little from the land. And sitting he taught the multitudes out of the ship.

4 Now when he had ceased to speak, he said to Simon: Launch out into the deep, and let down your nets for a draught.

5 And Simon answering said to him: Master, we have labored all the night, and have taken nothing: but at thy word I will let down the net.

6 And when they had done this, they enclosed a very great multitude of fishes, and their net broke.

7 And they beckoned to their partners that were in the other ship, that they should come and help them. And they came, and filled both the ships, so that they were almost sinking.

8 Which when Simon Peter saw, he fell down at Jesus' knees, saying: Depart from me, for I am a sinful man, O Lord.

9 For he was wholly astonished, and all that were with him, at the draught of the fishes which they had taken.

10 And so were also James and John the sons of Zebedee, who were Simon's partners. And Jesus saith to Simon: Fear not: from henceforth thou shalt catch men.

11 And having brought their ships to land, leaving all things, they followed him.

The Gospel of Luke presents a captivating story of faith and obedience. Jesus, surrounded by a crowd eager to hear his message, instructs Simon Peter to put out into deeper water and let down his nets for a catch. Peter, a seasoned fisherman, hesitates, pointing out their lack of success the previous night. Yet, in an act of faith, he obeys Jesus' command. The result is a miraculous catch, so abundant that their nets begin to tear. This miracle not only provides for the fishermen but also signifies the potential for abundant blessings when we follow Jesus' call.

Reflect & Respond:

- How does Isaiah's encounter with God inspire you to approach your own relationship with God?

- Consider the concept of faith in 1 Corinthians. What are some areas in your life where you need to strengthen your faith?

- The story of the miraculous catch highlights the importance of obedience. Is there a situation in your life where you are being called to step outside your comfort zone and trust in God's guidance?

Prayer:

Dear Heavenly Father, thank you for revealing yourself to us and calling us to follow you. Grant us the courage to answer your call, even when it feels challenging. Increase our faith and trust in you, and empower us to be instruments of your love and grace in the world. Amen.

Challenge:

This week, reflect on a personal call you may be feeling – a nudge to help someone in need, pursue a new direction, or simply deepen your faith. Take a step forward, even if it's small. Remember, even seemingly insignificant actions can have a ripple effect, and God can work wonders through our obedience.

Notes:_____

_____

_____

_____

_____

Sunday, February 16

- Sixth Sunday in Ordinary Time

First Reading: Jeremiah 17: 5-8

Responsorial Psalm: Psalms 1: 1-2, 3, 4 and 6

Second Reading: First Corinthians 15: 12, 16-20

Alleluia: Luke 6: 23ab

Gospel: Luke 6: 17, 20-26

Lectionary: 78

This Sixth Sunday in Ordinary Time invites us to contemplate true happiness, the importance of perspective, and the blessings that come with following Jesus' teachings.

Jeremiah on Trusting in the Lord (Jeremiah 17: 5-8):

5 Thus saith the Lord: Cursed be the man that trusteth in man, and maketh flesh his arm, and whose heart departeth from the Lord.

6 For he shall be like tamaric in the desert, and he shall not see when good shall come: but he shall dwell in dryness in the desert in a salt land, and not inhabited.

7 Blessed be the man that trusteth in the Lord, and the Lord shall be his confidence.

8 And he shall be as a tree that is planted by the waters, that spreadeth out its roots towards moisture: and it shall not fear when the heat cometh. And the leaf thereof shall be green, and in the time of drought it shall not be solicitous, neither shall it cease at any time to bring forth fruit.

The first reading from Jeremiah offers a powerful message about trusting in God. The prophet contrasts those who rely on human strength and fleeting pleasures with those who place their trust in the Lord. Jeremiah emphasizes that the one who trusts in God is like a flourishing tree, secure and well-watered, while those who rely on human strength are like withered shrubs in a desert. This passage reminds us that true security and happiness come from a deep connection with God.

Responsorial Psalm: Psalms 1: 1-2, 3, 4 and 6

R. (40:5a) Blessed are they who hope in the Lord.

1 Blessed is the man who hath not walked in the counsel of the ungodly, nor stood in the way of sinners, nor sat in the chair of pestilence.

2 But his will is in the law of the Lord, and on his law he shall meditate day and night.

R. Blessed are they who hope in the Lord.

3 And he shall be like a tree which is planted near the running waters, which shall bring forth its fruit, in due season.

And his leaf shall not fall off: and all whatsoever he shall do shall prosper.

R. Blessed are they who hope in the Lord.

4 Not so the wicked, not so: but like the dust, which the wind driveth from the face of the earth.

6 For the Lord knoweth the way of the just: and the way of the wicked shall perish.

R. Blessed are they who hope in the Lord.

The Hope of Resurrection (1 Corinthians 15: 12, 16-20):

12 Now if Christ be preached, that he arose again from the dead, how do some among you say, that there is no resurrection of the dead?

16 For if the dead rise not again, neither is Christ risen again.

17 And if Christ be not risen again, your faith is vain, for you are yet in your sins.

18 Then they also that are fallen asleep in Christ, are perished.

19 If in this life only we have hope in Christ, we are of all men most miserable.

20 But now Christ is risen from the dead, the firstfruits of them that sleep:

The passage from 1 Corinthians picks up on the theme of faith from last week. Paul emphasizes the centrality of Jesus' resurrection to the Christian faith. If Christ has not been raised, our faith is empty, and we offer no real hope. However, Paul assures the Corinthians that Christ has indeed been raised, conquering death and offering the promise of eternal life for all who believe.

Alleluia: Luke 6: 23ab

R. Alleluia, alleluia.

23ab Rejoice and be glad; your reward will be great in heaven.

R. Alleluia, alleluia.

The Beatitudes (Luke 6: 17, 20-26):

17 And coming down with them, he stood in a plain place, and the company of his disciples, and a very great multitude of people from all Judea and Jerusalem, and the sea coast both of Tyre and Sidon,

20 And he, lifting up his eyes on his disciples, said: Blessed are ye poor, for yours is the kingdom of God.

21 Blessed are ye that hunger now: for you shall be filled. Blessed are ye that weep now: for you shall laugh.

22 Blessed shall you be when men shall hate you, and when they shall separate you, and shall reproach you, and cast out your name as evil, for the Son of man's sake.

23 Be glad in that day and rejoice; for behold, your reward is great in heaven. For according to these things did their fathers to the prophets.

24 But woe to you that are rich: for you have your consolation.

25 Woe to you that are filled: for you shall hunger. Woe to you that

now laugh: for you shall mourn and weep.

26 Woe to you when men shall bless you: for according to these things did their fathers to the false prophets.

The Gospel of Luke presents the famous Beatitudes, some of the most well-known teachings of Jesus. Jesus proclaims blessings upon the poor, the hungry, the weeping, and the persecuted, challenging societal norms and offering a different perspective on happiness. He emphasizes that true joy comes not from material possessions or worldly success, but from living according to God's will and aligning oneself with his kingdom.

Reflect & Respond:

- How does Jeremiah's message about trusting in God challenge your own understanding of where you find security and happiness?

- Consider the concept of the resurrection in 1 Corinthians. How does the hope of eternal life impact your perspective on life's challenges?

- The Beatitudes offer a counterintuitive perspective on happiness. Is there an area in your life where you need to shift your focus from worldly pursuits to spiritual values?

Prayer:

Dear God, help us to see the world through your eyes and find true joy in following your path. Grant us the strength to trust in your promises and the wisdom to discern your will in our lives. May we live according to your teachings, so that our lives reflect your love and compassion. Amen.

Challenge:

This week, practice gratitude for the simple blessings in your life. Take some time each day to reflect on the good things, big or small, that bring you joy. Consider keeping a gratitude journal or sharing your appreciation with someone you love. By focusing on the positive, you can cultivate a more joyful and hopeful outlook.

Notes:_____

_____
_____
_____
_____
_____
_____
_____
_____
_____
_____
_____
_____
_____

_____
_____
_____
_____
_____
_____
_____
_____
_____
_____
_____
_____
_____
_____
_____
_____
_____
_____
_____
_____
_____
_____
_____
_____

Sunday, February 23

- Seventh Sunday in Ordinary Time

First Reading: First Samuel 26: 2, 7-9, 12-13, 22-23

Responsorial Psalm: Psalms 103: 1-2, 3-4, 8, 10, 12-13

Second Reading: First Corinthians 15: 45-49

Alleluia: John 13: 34

Gospel: Luke 6: 27-38

Lectionary: 81

This Seventh Sunday in Ordinary Time challenges us to extend love and compassion beyond our comfort zone, mirroring the boundless love of God.

David Shows Restraint (First Samuel 26: 2, 7-9, 12-13, 22-23):

2 Saul arose, and went down to the wilderness of Ziph, having with him three thousand chosen men of Israel, to seek David in the wilderness of Ziph.

7 So David and Abisai came to the people by night, and found Saul lying and sleeping in the tent, and his spear fixed in the ground at his head: and Abner and the people sleeping round about him.

8 And Abisai said to David: God hath shut up thy enemy this day into thy hands: now then I will run him through with my spear even to the earth at once, and there shall be no need of a second time.

9 And David said to Abisai: Kill him not: for who shall put forth his hand against the Lord's anointed, and shall be guiltless?

12 So David took the spear, and the cup of water which was at Saul's head, and they went away: and no man saw it, or knew it, or awaked, but they were all asleep, for a deep sleep from the Lord was fallen upon them.

13 And when David was gone over to the other side. and stood on the top of the hill afar off, and a good space was between them,

22 And David answering, said: Behold the king's spear: let one of the king's servants come over and fetch it.

23 And the Lord will reward every one according to his justice, and his faithfulness: for the Lord hath delivered thee this day into my hand, and I would not put forth my hand against the Lord's anointed.

The first reading sets the stage with a dramatic story from the book of Samuel. David, on the run from King Saul who seeks to kill him, finds Saul sleeping unguarded in his camp. David has the opportunity to eliminate his enemy, yet he chooses to show mercy. This act of restraint reflects God's own compassion and forgiveness, even towards those who oppose him.

Responsorial Psalm: Psalms 103: 1-2, 3-4, 8, 10, 12-13

R. (8a) The Lord is kind and merciful.

1 Bless the Lord, O my soul: and let all that is within me bless his holy name.

2 Bless the Lord, O my soul, and never forget all he hath done for thee.

R. The Lord is kind and merciful.

3 Who forgiveth all thy iniquities: who healeth all thy diseases.

4 Who redeemeth thy life from destruction: who crowneth thee with mercy and compassion.

R. The Lord is kind and merciful.

8 The Lord is compassionate and merciful: longsuffering and plenteous in mercy.

10 He hath not dealt with us according to our sins: nor rewarded us according to our iniquities.

R. The Lord is kind and merciful.

12 As far as the east is from the west, so far hath he removed our iniquities from us.

13 As a father hath compassion on his children, so hath the Lord compassion on them that fear him:

R. The Lord is kind and merciful.

Transformed by Love (First Corinthians 15: 45-49):

45 The first man Adam was made into a living soul; the last Adam into a quickening spirit.

46 Yet that was not first which is spiritual, but that which is natural; afterwards that which is spiritual.

47 The first man was of the earth, earthly: the second man, from heaven, heavenly.

48 Such as is the earthly, such also are the earthly: and such as is the heavenly, such also are they that are heavenly.

49 Therefore as we have borne the image of the earthly, let us bear also the image of the heavenly.

The passage from 1 Corinthians delves deeper into the transformative power of love. Paul speaks of Adam and Christ as contrasting figures. Adam, the first man, brought sin and death into the world. Christ, the new Adam, brings new life and the promise of a transformed existence. Through Christ, we are no longer bound by our earthly limitations but can be clothed with the imperishable, reflecting God's love in all we do.

Alleluia: John 13: 34

R. Alleluia, alleluia.

34 I give you a new commandment, says the Lord: love one another as I have loved you.

R. Alleluia, alleluia.

Love Your Enemies (Luke 6: 27-38):

27 But I say to you that hear: Love your enemies, do good to them that hate you.

28 Bless them that curse you, and pray for them that calumniate you.

29 And to him that striketh thee on the one cheek, offer also the other. And him that taketh away from thee thy cloak, forbid not to take thy coat also.

30 Give to every one that asketh thee, and of him that taketh away thy goods, ask them not again.

31 And as you would that men should do to you, do you also to them in like manner.

32 And if you love them that love you, what thanks are to you? for sinners also love those that love them.

33 And if you do good to them who do good to you, what thanks are to you? for sinners also do this.

34 And if you lend to them of whom you hope to receive, what thanks are to you? for sinners also lend to sinners, for to receive as much.

35 But love ye your enemies: do good, and lend, hoping for nothing thereby: and your reward shall be great, and you shall be the sons of the Highest; for he is kind to the unthankful, and to the evil.

36 Be ye therefore merciful, as your Father also is merciful.

37 Judge not, and you shall not be judged. Condemn not, and you shall not be condemned. Forgive, and you shall be forgiven.

38 Give, and it shall be given to you: good measure and pressed down and shaken together and running over shall they give into your bosom. For with the same measure that you shall mete withal, it shall be measured to you again.

The Gospel of Luke presents some of Jesus' most challenging teachings. He instructs his followers to love their enemies, do good to those who hate them, bless those who curse them, and pray for those who mistreat them. Jesus encourages his disciples to extend compassion and generosity beyond those who deserve it, mirroring the way God himself loves unconditionally.

Reflect & Respond:

- How does the story of David and Saul challenge your own understanding of forgiveness and showing mercy?

- Consider the concept of transformation in 1 Corinthians. How can you allow God's love to transform your own thoughts, words, and actions?

- Jesus' teaching to love our enemies is difficult. Is there someone in your life you need to forgive or show kindness towards, even if it's challenging?

Prayer:

Dear God, thank you for your boundless love and compassion. Grant us the strength to forgive those who have wronged us and to extend love even to our enemies. Help us to see the world through your eyes and live according to your teachings. May our hearts be transformed by your love, and may we be instruments of your peace in the world. Amen.

Challenge:

This week, practice a random act of kindness for someone you don't know well or who may have even been unkind to you in the past. It could be a simple smile, a helping hand, or a word of encouragement. Remember, even small gestures can have a ripple effect and spread God's love in unexpected ways.

Notes:_____
_____
_____
_____
_____
_____
_____
_____
_____
_____
_____

March 2025

Sunday, March 2

- Eighth Sunday in Ordinary Time

First Reading: Sirach 27: 4-7

Responsorial Psalm: Psalms 92: 2-3, 13-14, 15-16

Second Reading: First Corinthians 15: 54-58

Alleluia: Philippians 2: 15d, 16a

Gospel: Luke 6: 39-45

Lectionary: 84

This Eighth Sunday in Ordinary Time invites us to cultivate discernment, to see the world clearly, and to act with wisdom and compassion.

The Importance of Wisdom (Sirach 27: 4-7):

4 As when one sifteth with a sieve, the dust will remain: so will the perplexity of a man in his thoughts.

5 The furnace trieth the potter's vessels, and the trial of affliction just men.

6 Be the dressing of a tree sheweth the fruit thereof, so a word out of the thought of the heart of man.

7 Praise not a man before he speaketh, for this is the trial of men.

The first reading, from the book of Sirach, emphasizes the importance of wisdom. The author encourages us to test our friends as a silversmith tests silver, discerning their true character and intentions. True wisdom allows us to see through facades and make wise choices in our relationships.

Responsorial Psalm: Psalms 92: 2-3, 13-14, 15-16

R. (2a) Lord, it is good to give thanks to you.

2 It is good to give praise to the Lord: and to sing to thy name, O most High.

3 To shew forth thy mercy in the morning, and thy truth in the night:

R. Lord, it is good to give thanks to you.

13 The just shall flourish like the palm tree: he shall grow up like the cedar of Libanus.

14 They that are planted in the house of the Lord shall flourish in the courts of the house of our God.

R. Lord, it is good to give thanks to you.

15 They shall still increase in a fruitful old age: and shall be well treated,

16 That they may shew, That the Lord our God is righteous, and there is no iniquity in him.

R. Lord, it is good to give thanks to you.

Victory Over Death (First Corinthians 15: 54-58):

54 And when this mortal hath put on immortality, then shall come to pass the saying that is written: Death is swallowed up in victory.

55 O death, where is thy victory? O death, where is thy sting?

56 Now the sting of death is sin: and the power of sin is the law.

57 But thanks be to God, who hath given us the victory through our Lord Jesus Christ.

58 Therefore, my beloved brethren, be ye steadfast and unmoveable; always abounding in the work of the Lord, knowing that your labour is not in vain in the Lord.

The passage from 1 Corinthians picks up on the theme of transformation from last week. Paul speaks of the ultimate victory over death through Christ. He describes the transformation that will occur when the perishable puts on the imperishable and the mortal puts on immortality. Through faith in Christ, we can look forward to a future free from death's sting.

Alleluia: Philippians 2: 15d, 16a

R. Alleluia, alleluia.

15d, 16a Shine like lights in the world as you hold on to the word of life.

R. Alleluia, alleluia.

Blind Leading the Blind (Luke 6: 39-45):

39 And he spoke also to them a similitude: Can the blind lead the blind? do they not both fall into the ditch?

40 The disciple is not above his master: but every one shall be perfect, if he be as his master.

41 And why seest thou the mote in thy brother's eye: but the beam that is in thy own eye thou considerest not?

42 Or how canst thou say to thy brother: Brother, let me pull the mote out of thy eye, when thou thyself seest not the beam in thy own eye? Hypocrite, cast first the beam out of thy own eye; and then shalt thou see clearly to take out the mote from thy brother's eye.

43 For there is no good tree that bringeth forth evil fruit; nor an evil tree that bringeth forth good fruit.

44 For every tree is known by its fruit. For men do not gather figs from thorns; nor from a bramble bush do they gather the grape.

45 A good man out of the good treasure of his heart bringeth forth that which is good: and an evil man out of the evil treasure bringeth forth that which is evil. For out of the abundance of the heart the mouth speaketh.

The Gospel of Luke presents some of Jesus' teachings on discernment and judgment. He uses a parable to illustrate the importance of seeing clearly. A blind person cannot lead another blind person; they will both fall. Jesus challenges his listeners to remove the log from their own eye before trying to remove the speck from their brother's eye. In other words, we must first address our own shortcomings before judging others.

Reflect & Respond:

- How does the passage from Sirach challenge you to be more discerning in your relationships?

- Consider the concept of victory over death in 1 Corinthians. How does this concept impact your perspective on life's challenges?

- Jesus' teaching about the blind leading the blind emphasizes self-awareness. Is there an area in your life where you need to work on your own shortcomings before criticizing others?

Prayer:

Dear God, grant us the wisdom to discern truth from deception and the courage to see ourselves and others clearly. Help us to remove the obstacles from our own vision so that we can extend compassion and understanding to those around us. May your light guide our steps and your love transform our hearts. Amen.

Challenge:

This week, commit to practicing active listening in your conversations. Pay close attention to what others are saying, both verbally and nonverbally. Try to see things from their perspective before offering judgment or advice. By truly listening, you can gain a deeper understanding of those around you and build stronger relationships.

Notes:_____
_____
_____
_____
_____

Sunday, March 9

- First Sunday of Lent

First Reading: Deuteronomy 26: 4-10

Responsorial Psalm: Psalms 91: 1-2, 10-11, 12-13, 14-15

Second Reading: Romans 10: 8-13

Verse Before the Gospel: Matthew 4: 4b

Gospel: Luke 4: 1-13

Lectionary: 24

Today marks the beginning of Lent, a sacred season of reflection, repentance, and preparation for the Easter celebration. The readings for the First Sunday of Lent set the tone for this introspective journey.

Remembering God's Deliverance (Deuteronomy 26: 4-10):

4 And the priest taking the basket at thy hand, shall set it before the altar of the Lord thy God:

5 And thou shalt speak thus in the sight of the Lord thy God: The Syrian pursued my father, who went down into Egypt, and sojourned there in a very small number, and grew into a nation great and strong and of an infinite multitude.

6 And the Egyptians afflicted us, and persecuted us, laying on us most grievous burdens:

7 And we cried to the Lord God of our fathers: who heard us, and looked down upon our affliction, and labour, and distress:

8 And brought us out of Egypt with a strong hand, and a stretched out arm, with great terror, with signs and wonders:

9 And brought us into this place, and gave us this land flowing with milk and honey.

10 And therefore now I offer the firstfruits of the land which the

Lord hath given me. And thou shalt leave them in the sight of the Lord thy God, adoring the Lord thy God.

The first reading from Deuteronomy recounts the Israelites' story of liberation from slavery in Egypt. They are called to remember the challenges they faced and God's faithfulness in delivering them. This passage serves as a reminder of our own need for God's grace and the importance of acknowledging his presence in our lives.

Responsorial Psalm: Psalms 91: 1-2, 10-11, 12-13, 14-15

R. (15b) Be with me, Lord, when I am in trouble.

1 He that dwelleth in the aid of the most High, shall abide under the protection of the God of Jacob.

2 He shall say to the Lord: Thou art my protector, and my refuge: my God, in him will I trust.

R. Be with me, Lord, when I am in trouble.

10 There shall no evil come to thee: nor shall the scourge come near thy dwelling.

11 For he hath given his angels charge over thee; to keep thee in all thy ways.

R. Be with me, Lord, when I am in trouble.

12 In their hands they shall bear thee up: lest thou dash thy foot against a stone.

13 Thou shalt walk upon the asp and the basilisk: and thou shalt trample under foot the lion and the dragon.

R. Be with me, Lord, when I am in trouble.

14 Because he hoped in me I will deliver him: I will protect him because he hath known my name.

15 He shall cry to me, and I will hear him: I am with him in tribulation, I will deliver him, and I will glorify him.

R. Be with me, Lord, when I am in trouble.

Proclaiming the Message of Salvation (Romans 10: 8-13):

8 But what saith the scripture? The word is nigh thee, even in thy mouth, and in thy heart. This is the word of faith, which we preach.

9 For if thou confess with thy mouth the Lord Jesus, and believe in thy heart that God hath raised him up from the dead, thou shalt be saved.

10 For, with the heart, we believe unto justice; but, with the mouth, confession is made unto salvation.

11 For the scripture saith: Whosoever believeth in him, shall not be confounded.

12 For there is no distinction of the Jew and the Greek: for the same is Lord over all, rich unto all that call upon him.

13 For whosoever shall call upon the name of the Lord, shall be saved.

The passage from Romans offers a message of hope and inclusion. Paul emphasizes that the word of salvation is near us, readily available to all who believe. He highlights the importance of confessing Jesus as Lord and believing in his resurrection for salvation. This message transcends religious boundaries, offering the promise of God's love to everyone.

Verse Before the Gospel: Matthew 4: 4b

4b One does not live on bread alone, but on every word that comes forth from the mouth of God.

Temptation in the Wilderness (Luke 4: 1-13):

1 And Jesus being full of the Holy Ghost, returned from the Jordan, and was led by the Spirit into the desert,

2 For the space of forty days; and was tempted by the devil. And he ate nothing in those days; and when they were ended, he was hungry.

3 And the devil said to him: If thou be the Son of God, say to this stone that it be made bread.

4 And Jesus answered him: It is written, that Man liveth not by bread alone, but by every word of God.

5 And the devil led him into a high mountain, and shewed him all the kingdoms of the world in a moment of time;

6 And he said to him: To thee will I give all this power, and the glory of them; for to me they are delivered, and to whom I will, I give them.

7 If thou therefore wilt adore before me, all shall be thine.

8 And Jesus answering said to him: It is written: Thou shalt adore the Lord thy God, and him only shalt thou serve.

9 And he brought him to Jerusalem, and set him on a pinnacle of the temple, and he said to him: If thou be the Son of God, cast thyself from hence.

10 For it is written, that He hath given his angels charge over thee, that they keep thee.

11 And that in their hands they shall bear thee up, lest perhaps thou dash thy foot against a stone.

12 And Jesus answering, said to him: It is said: Thou shalt not tempt the Lord thy God.

13 And all the temptation being ended, the devil departed from him for a time.

The Gospel of Luke recounts Jesus' experience of temptation in the wilderness following his baptism. The Holy Spirit leads Jesus into the wilderness, where he is tempted by the devil. Jesus, filled with the Holy Spirit, resists these temptations, demonstrating his unwavering faith and obedience to God's will. This passage reminds us that even Jesus faced temptation, but through his reliance on God, he emerged victorious.

Reflect & Respond:

- How does the story of the Israelites in Deuteronomy resonate with your own experiences of God's deliverance in your life?

- Consider the message of salvation in Romans. How can you share this message of hope with others?

- Jesus' experience in the wilderness reminds us that we will all face temptation. What are some of the temptations you struggle with? How can you rely on God's strength to resist them?

Prayer:

Almighty God, as we enter the season of Lent, guide us on a journey of introspection and renewal. Help us to remember your faithfulness in our lives and to acknowledge our need for your grace. Grant us the strength to resist temptation and to follow your will with unwavering faith. May this Lent be a time of transformation, leading us closer to you and a deeper understanding of your love. Amen.

Challenge:

This week, consider what you want to focus on during Lent. Is it prayer, reflection, giving to charity, or simply spending less time on distractions? Choose a specific practice to incorporate into your daily routine throughout Lent. Remember, even small changes can make a big difference on your spiritual journey.

Notes:_____
_____
_____
_____
_____
_____
_____
_____
_____
_____
_____
_____
_____
_____
_____
_____
_____

Sunday, March 16

- Second Sunday of Lent

First Reading: Genesis 15: 5-12, 17-18

Responsorial Psalm: Psalms 27: 1, 7-8, 8-9, 13-14

Second Reading: Philippians 3: 17 – 4: 1 or 3: 20 – 4: 1

Verse Before the Gospel: Matthew 17: 5

Gospel: Luke 9: 28b-36

Lectionary: 27

This Second Sunday of Lent offers a moment of reflection amidst the season of sacrifice and introspection. The readings provide a glimpse of God's glory, a promise of what awaits those who remain faithful.

Covenant with Abram (Genesis 15: 5-12, 17-18):

5 And he brought him forth abroad, and said to him: Look up to heaven and number the stars, if thou canst. And he said to him: So shall thy seed be.

6 Abram believed God, and it was reputed to him unto justice.

7 And he said to him: I am the Lord who brought thee out from Ur of the Chaldees, to give thee this land, and that thou mightest possess it.

8 But he said: Lord God, whereby may I know that I shall possess it?

9 And the Lord answered, and said: Take me a cow of three years old, and a she goat of three years, and a ram of three years, a turtle also, and a pigeon.

10 And he took all these, and divided them in the midst, and laid the two pieces of each one against the other; but the birds he divided not.

11 And the fowls came down upon the carcasses, and Abram drove them away.

12 And when the sun was setting, a deep sleep fell upon Abram, and a great and darksome horror seized upon him.

17 And when the sun was set, there arose a dark mist, and there appeared a smoking furnace and a lamp of fire passing between those divisions.

18 That day God made a covenant with Abram, saying: To thy seed will I give this land, from the river of Egypt even to the great river Euphrates.

The first reading from Genesis recounts God's covenant with Abram. God assures Abram of his countless descendants and promises him a land inheritance. Abram responds with faith, believing in God's promises even though he is childless at the time. This passage highlights the importance of faith and God's faithfulness to his promises.

Responsorial Psalm: Psalms 27: 1, 7-8, 8-9, 13-14

R. (1a) The Lord is my light and my salvation.

1 The Lord is my light and my salvation, whom shall I fear?

The Lord is the protector of my life: of whom shall I be afraid?

R. The Lord is my light and my salvation.

7 Hear, O Lord, my voice, with which I have cried to thee: have mercy on me and hear me.

8ab My heart hath said to thee: My face hath sought thee.

R. The Lord is my light and my salvation.

8c Thy face, O Lord, will I still seek.

9 Turn not away thy face from me; decline not in thy wrath from thy servant. Be thou my helper, forsake me not; do not thou despise me, O God my Saviour.

R. The Lord is my light and my salvation.

13 I believe to see the good things of the Lord in the land of the living.

14 Expect the Lord, do manfully, and let thy heart take courage, and wait thou for the Lord.

R. The Lord is my light and my salvation.

Living as Citizens of Heaven (Philippians 3: 17 - 4: 1 or 3: 20 - 4: 1):

17 Be ye followers of me, brethren, and observe them who walk so as you have our model.

18 For many walk, of whom I have told you often (and now tell you weeping), that they are enemies of the cross of Christ;

19 Whose end is destruction; whose God is their belly; and whose glory is in their shame; who mind earthly things.

20 But our conversation is in heaven; from whence also we look for the Saviour, our Lord Jesus Christ,

21 Who will reform the body of our lowness, made like to the body of his glory, according to the operation whereby also he is able to subdue all things unto himself.

4:1 Therefore, my dearly beloved brethren, and most desired, my joy and my crown; so stand fast in the Lord, my dearly beloved.

Or

20 But our conversation is in heaven; from whence also we look for the Saviour, our Lord Jesus Christ,

21 Who will reform the body of our lowness, made like to the body of his glory, according to the operation whereby also he is able to subdue all things unto himself.

4:1 Therefore, my dearly beloved brethren, and most desired, my joy and my crown; so stand fast in the Lord, my dearly beloved.

The passage from Philippians offers guidance for Christian living. Paul encourages the Philippians to live as worthy citizens of heaven, while reminding them of their earthly limitations. He emphasizes that our true home is in heaven, and we should strive to live according to heavenly values.

Verse Before the Gospel: Matthew 17: 5

5 From the shining cloud the Father's voice is heard: This is my beloved Son, hear him.

28b Jesus took Peter, and James, and John, and went up into a mountain to pray.

29 And whilst he prayed, the shape of his countenance was altered, and his raiment became white and glittering.

30 And behold two men were talking with him. And they were Moses and Elias,

31 Appearing in majesty. And they spoke of his decease that he should accomplish in Jerusalem.

32 But Peter and they that were with him were heavy with sleep. And waking, they saw his glory, and the two men that stood with him.

33 And it came to pass, that as they were departing from him, Peter saith to Jesus: Master, it is good for us to be here; and let us make three tabernacles, one for thee, and one for Moses, and one for Elias; not knowing what he said.

34 And as he spoke these things, there came a cloud, and overshadowed them; and they were afraid, when they entered into the cloud.

35 And a voice came out of the cloud, saying: This is my beloved Son; hear him.

36 And whilst the voice was uttered, Jesus was found alone. And they held their peace, and told no man in those days any of these things which they had seen.

The Gospel of Luke presents the story of the Transfiguration. Jesus takes Peter, James, and John up a mountain to pray. While he prays, his appearance is transformed, radiating divine light. Moses and Elijah appear, representing the Law and the Prophets, and speak with Jesus about his coming departure. A voice from heaven proclaims Jesus as God's Son, the Chosen One. This event offers a glimpse of Jesus' divine glory and foreshadows his victory over death.

Reflect & Respond:

- How does the story of God's covenant with Abram inspire you to have faith in God's promises?

- Consider the concept of heavenly citizenship in Philippians. How can you live your daily life in a way that reflects your heavenly identity?

- The Transfiguration reveals a glimpse of Jesus' glory. How does this event impact your understanding of Jesus' identity and mission?

Prayer:

Dear God, thank you for the gift of faith and the promise of eternal life. Grant us the strength to remain faithful during challenging times, trusting in your goodness and your plan for our lives. May the glimpse of your glory we receive through the Transfiguration story fill us with hope and inspire us to live according to your will. Amen.

Challenge:

This week, spend some time in prayer or reflection considering your own values and priorities. How do they align with your faith? Are there areas where you can make adjustments to live a more Christ-centered life?

Notes:_____
_____
_____
_____
_____
_____
_____
_____
_____
_____
_____
_____
_____
_____
_____
_____
_____
_____
_____
_____

Sunday, March 23

- **Third Sunday of Lent**

First Reading: Exodus 3: 1-8a, 13-15

Responsorial Psalm: Psalms 103: 1-2, 3-4, 6-7, 8, 11

Second Reading: First Corinthians 10: 1-6, 10-12

Verse Before the Gospel: Matthew 4: 17

Gospel: Luke 13: 1-9

Lectionary: 30

This Third Sunday of Lent emphasizes the importance of repentance, perseverance, and the ongoing call to bear fruit in our lives. The readings offer a message of hope alongside a reminder of the need for action and transformation.

The Burning Bush and Moses' Call (Exodus 3: 1-8a, 13-15):

1 Now Moses fed the sheep of Jethro his father in law, the priest of Madian: and he drove the flock to the inner parts of the desert, and came to the mountain of God, Horeb.

2 And the Lord appeared to him in a flame of fire out of the midst of a bush: and he saw that the bush was on fire and was not burnt.

3 And Moses said: I will go and see this great sight, why the bush is not burnt.

4 And when the Lord saw that he went forward to see, he called to him out of the midst of the bush, and said: Moses, Moses. And he answered: Here I am.

5 And he said: Come not nigh hither, put off the shoes from thy feet: for the place whereon thou standest is holy ground.

6 And he said: I am the God of thy father, the God of Abraham, the God of Isaac, and the God of Jacob. Moses hid his face: for he durst not look at God.

7 And the Lord said to him: I have seen the affliction of my people in Egypt, and I have heard their cry because of the rigour of them that are over the works:

8 And knowing their sorrow, I am come down to deliver them out of the hands of the Egyptians, and to bring them out of that land into a good and spacious land, into a land that floweth with milk and honey.

13 Moses said to God: Lo, I shall go to the children of Israel, and say to them: The God of your fathers hath sent me to you. If they should say to me: What is his name? what shall I say to them?

14 God said to Moses: I AM WHO AM. He said: Thus shalt thou say to the children of Israel: HE WHO IS, hath sent me to you.

15 And God said again to Moses: Thus shalt thou say to the children of Israel: The Lord God of your fathers, the God of Abraham, the God of Isaac, and the God of Jacob, hath sent me to you: This is my name for ever, and this is my memorial unto all generations.

The first reading from Exodus recounts the story of Moses encountering God at the burning bush. God commissions Moses to lead the Israelites out of slavery in Egypt. Moses expresses hesitation and self-doubt, but God assures him of his presence and guidance. This passage highlights God's initiative in reaching out to his people and the importance of responding to his call, even when we feel inadequate.

Responsorial Psalm: Psalms 103: 1-2, 3-4, 6-7, 8, 11

R. (8a) The Lord is kind and merciful.

1 Bless the Lord, O my soul: and let all that is within me bless his holy name.

2 Bless the Lord, O my soul, and never forget all he hath done for thee.

R. The Lord is kind and merciful.

3 Who forgiveth all thy iniquities: who healeth all thy diseases.

4 Who redeemeth thy life from destruction: who crowneth thee with mercy and compassion.

R. **The Lord is kind and merciful.**

6 The Lord doth mercies, and judgment for all that suffer wrong.

7 He hath made his ways known to Moses: his wills to the children of Israel.

R. **The Lord is kind and merciful.**

8 The Lord is compassionate and merciful: longsuffering and plenteous in mercy.

11 For according to the height of the heaven above the earth: he hath strengthened his mercy towards them that fear him.

R. **The Lord is kind and merciful.**

Learning from the Israelites' Journey (First Corinthians 10: 1-6, 10-12):

1 For I would not have you ignorant, brethren, that our fathers were all under the cloud, and all passed through the sea.

2 And all in Moses were baptized, in the cloud, and in the sea:

3 And did all eat the same spiritual food,

4 And all drank the same spiritual drink; (and they drank of the spiritual rock that followed them, and the rock was Christ.)

5 But with most of them God was not well pleased: for they were overthrown in the desert.

6 Now these things were done in a figure of us, that we should not covet evil things as they also coveted.

10 Neither do you murmur: as some of them murmured, and were destroyed by the destroyer.

11 Now all these things happened to them in figure: and they are written for our correction, upon whom the ends of the world are come.

12 Wherefore he that thinketh himself to stand, let him take heed lest he fall.

The passage from 1 Corinthians uses the story of the Israelites' wandering in the wilderness as a cautionary tale. The Corinthians are reminded of the Israelites' grumbling, idolatry, and disobedience, which resulted in punishment from God. Paul emphasizes that these things happened as examples for us, so that we can learn from their mistakes and avoid repeating them.

Verse Before the Gospel: Matthew 4: 17

17 Repent, says the Lord; the kingdom of heaven is at hand.

The Barren Fig Tree (Luke 13: 1-9):

1 And there were present, at that very time, some that told him of the Galileans, whose blood Pilate had mingled with their sacrifices.

2 And he answering, said to them: Think you that these Galileans were sinners above all the men of Galilee, because they suffered such things?

3 No, I say to you: but unless you shall do penance, you shall all likewise perish.

4 Or those eighteen upon whom the tower fell in Siloe, and slew them: think you, that they also were debtors above all the men that dwelt in Jerusalem?

5 No, I say to you; but except you do penance, you shall all likewise perish.

6 He spoke also this parable: A certain man had a fig tree planted in his vineyard, and he came seeking fruit on it, and found none.

7 And he said to the dresser of the vineyard: Behold, for these three years I come seeking fruit on this fig tree, and I find none. Cut it done therefore: why cumbereth it the ground?

8 But he answering, said to him: Lord, let it alone this year also, until I dig about it, and dung it.

9 And if happily it bear fruit: but if not, then after that thou shalt cut it down.

The Gospel of Luke presents the parable of the barren fig tree. The owner of a vineyard wants to cut down a fig tree that is not producing fruit, but the caretaker asks for one more year to see if it can be revived through careful tending. Jesus interprets this parable as a call to repentance. We are all called to bear fruit in our lives, and God offers us opportunities to improve. However, if we continue to be unproductive, there will be consequences.

Reflect & Respond:

- How does the story of Moses encountering God inspire you to respond to God's call in your own life?

- Consider the message in 1 Corinthians. Is there an area in your life where you need to repent or make a change to avoid repeating past mistakes?

- The parable of the barren fig tree is a call to bear fruit. What kind of "fruit" do you want to produce in your life? What steps can you take to cultivate this fruit?

Prayer:

Dear God, grant us the courage to confront our shortcomings and the humility to seek your forgiveness. Help us to learn from the mistakes of the past and to use this Lenten season as an opportunity for genuine renewal. May we bear fruit that reflects your love and grace in the world. Amen.

Challenge:

This week, commit to an act of kindness or service to someone in need. This could be anything from helping a neighbor to volunteering at a local charity. By reaching out to others, we not only bless them but also cultivate the fruit of compassion and love in our own lives.

Notes:_____
_____
_____
_____
_____

Sunday, March 30

- Fourth Sunday of Lent

First Reading: Joshua 5: 9a, 10-12

Responsorial Psalm: Psalms 34: 2-3, 4-5, 6-7

Second Reading: Second Corinthians 5: 17-21

Verse Before the Gospel: Luke 15: 18

Gospel: Luke 15: 1-3, 11-32

Lectionary: 33

This Fourth Sunday of Lent, also known as Laetare Sunday, offers a moment of joy and hope amidst the season of sacrifice. The readings celebrate God's extravagant love, his forgiveness, and the promise of reconciliation.

Passover After the Crossing (Joshua 5: 9a, 10-12):

9a The Lord said to Josue: This day have I taken away from you the reproach of Egypt.

10 And the children of Israel abode in Galgal, and they kept the phase on the fourteenth day of the month, at evening, in the plains of Jericho:

11 And they ate on the next day unleavened bread of the corn of the land, and frumenty of the same year.

12 And the manna ceased after they ate of the corn of the land, neither did the children of Israel use that food any more, but they ate of the corn of the present year of the land of Chanaan.

The first reading from Joshua recounts the Israelites celebrating Passover after crossing the Jordan River. This celebration signifies a new beginning for the people of God, a fresh start after their time of wandering in the wilderness.

R. (9a) Taste and see the goodness of the Lord.

2 I will bless the Lord at all times, his praise shall be always in my mouth.

3 In the Lord shall my soul be praised: let the meek hear and rejoice.

R. Taste and see the goodness of the Lord.

4 O magnify the Lord with me; and let us extol his name together.

5 I sought the Lord, and he heard me; and he delivered me from all my troubles.

R. Taste and see the goodness of the Lord.

6 Come ye to him and be enlightened: and your faces shall not be confounded.

7 This poor man cried, and the Lord heard him: and saved him out of all his troubles.

R. Taste and see the goodness of the Lord.

Reconciliation Through Christ (Second Corinthians 5: 17-21):

17 If then any be in Christ a new creature, the old things are passed away, behold all things are made new.

18 But all things are of God, who hath reconciled us to himself by Christ; and hath given to us the ministry of reconciliation.

19 For God indeed was in Christ, reconciling the world to himself, not imputing to them their sins; and he hath placed in us the word of reconciliation.

20 For Christ therefore we are ambassadors, God as it were exhorting by us. For Christ, we beseech you, be reconciled to God.

21 Him, who knew no sin, he hath made sin for us, that we might be made the justice of God in him.

The passage from 2 Corinthians emphasizes the transformative power of Christ's love. Paul speaks of a new creation in Christ, where the old has gone and the new has come. We are reconciled to God through Christ, becoming ambassadors for him, urging others to be reconciled as well.

Verse Before the Gospel: Luke 15: 18

18 I will get up and go to my Father and shall say to him: Father, I have sinned against heaven and against you.

The Parable of the Lost Son (Luke 15: 1-3, 11-32):

1 Now the publicans and sinners drew near unto him to hear him.

2 And the Pharisees and the scribes murmured, saying: This man receiveth sinners, and eateth with them.

3 And he spoke to them this parable, saying:

11 And he said: A certain man had two sons:

12 And the younger of them said to his father: Father, give me the portion of substance that falleth to me. And he divided unto them his substance.

13 And not many days after, the younger son, gathering all together, went abroad into a far country: and there wasted his substance, living riotously.

14 And after he had spent all, there came a mighty famine in that country; and he began to be in want.

15 And he went and cleaved to one of the citizens of that country. And he sent him into his farm to feed swine.

16 And he would fain have filled his belly with the husks the swine did eat; and no man gave unto him.

17 And returning to himself, he said: How many hired servants in my father's house abound with bread, and I here perish with hunger?

18 I will arise, and will go to my father, and say to him: Father, I have sinned against heaven, and before thee:

19 I am not worthy to be called thy son: make me as one of thy hired servants.

20 And rising up he came to his father. And when he was yet a great way off, his father saw him, and was moved with compassion, and running to him fell upon his neck, and kissed him.

21 And the son said to him: Father, I have sinned against heaven, and before thee, I am not now worthy to be called thy son.

22 And the father said to his servants: Bring forth quickly the first robe, and put it on him, and put a ring on his hand, and shoes on his feet:

23 And bring hither the fatted calf, and kill it, and let us eat and make merry:

24 Because this my son was dead, and is come to life again: was lost, and is found. And they began to be merry.

25 Now his elder son was in the field, and when he came and drew nigh to the house, he heard music and dancing:

26 And he called one of the servants, and asked what these things meant.

27 And he said to him: Thy brother is come, and thy father hath killed the fatted calf, because he hath received him safe.

28 And he was angry, and would not go in. His father therefore coming out began to entreat him.

29 And he answering, said to his father: Behold, for so many years do I serve thee, and I have never transgressed thy commandment, and yet thou hast never given me a kid to make merry with my friends:

30 But as soon as this thy son is come, who hath devoured his substance with harlots, thou hast killed for him the fatted calf.

31 But he said to him: Son, thou art always with me, and all I have is thine.

32 But it was fit that we should make merry and be glad, for this thy brother was dead and is come to life again; he was lost, and is found.

The Gospel of Luke presents the beloved Parable of the Lost Son. This story portrays God's love as unconditional and all-encompassing. The father welcomes back his younger son with open arms, celebrating his return even though he has squandered his inheritance. The parable contrasts the joy of the forgiving father with the resentment of the older son, who represents a self-righteous attitude.

Reflect & Respond:

- How does the story of the Israelites celebrating Passover inspire hope for new beginnings in your own life?

- Consider the concept of reconciliation in 2 Corinthians. Have you been reconciled to someone you were estranged from? Is there a relationship that needs mending in your life?

- The Parable of the Lost Son highlights God's extravagant love. How can you experience this love more fully in your own life? How can you share this love with others?

Prayer:

Dear God, thank you for your boundless love and mercy. Grant us the courage to admit our shortcomings and seek your forgiveness. Help us to be instruments of reconciliation in our relationships, reflecting your love to the world. May we experience the joy of your extravagant love and share it with all those we encounter. Amen.

Challenge:

This week, consider someone you may need to forgive or reconcile with. This could be a friend, family member, or even someone you don't know well but have had a disagreement with. Take a step towards reconciliation, even if it's just a small gesture or a heartfelt conversation. Remember, forgiveness and reconciliation can bring healing and joy to all involved.

Notes:_____
_____
_____

_____
_____
_____

April 2025

Sunday, April 6

- ## Fifth Sunday of Lent

First Reading: Ezekiel 37: 12-14

Responsorial Psalm: Psalms 130: 1-2, 3-4, 5-6, 7-8

Second Reading: Romans 8: 8-11

Verse Before the Gospel: John 11: 25a, 26

Gospel: John 11: 1-45

Lectionary: 34

This Fifth Sunday of Lent confronts us with the reality of death while offering a powerful message of hope and the promise of resurrection. The readings point towards Jesus' ultimate victory over death, foreshadowing his own resurrection to come.

The Valley of Dry Bones (Ezekiel 37: 12-14):

12 Therefore prophesy, and say to them: Thus saith the Lord God: Behold I will open your graves, and will bring you out of your sepulchres, O my people: and will bring you into the land of Israel.

13 And you shall know that I am the Lord, when I shall have opened your sepulchres, and shall have brought you out of your graves, O my people:

14 And shall have put my spirit in you, and you shall live, and I shall make you rest upon your own land: and you shall know that I the Lord have spoken, and done it, saith the Lord God:

The first reading from Ezekiel presents a vivid image of the prophet being brought to a valley filled with dry bones. God asks Ezekiel, "Son of man, can these bones live?" Ezekiel acknowledges that only God knows. God then breathes life into the bones, and they come together to form a vast army.

This passage symbolizes God's power over death and his ability to bring new life.

Responsorial Psalm: Psalms 130: 1-2, 3-4, 5-6, 7-8

R. (7bc) **With the Lord there is mercy and fullness of redemption.**

1 Out of the depths I have cried to thee, O Lord:

2 Lord, hear my voice. Let thy ears be attentive to the voice of my supplication.

R. **With the Lord there is mercy and fullness of redemption.**

3 If thou, O Lord, wilt mark iniquities: Lord, who shall stand it.

4 For with thee there is merciful forgiveness: and by reason of thy law, I have waited for thee, O Lord. My soul hath relied on his word:

R. **With the Lord there is mercy and fullness of redemption.**

5 My soul hath hoped in the Lord.

6 From the morning watch even until night, let Israel hope in the Lord.

R. **With the Lord there is mercy and fullness of redemption.**

7 Because with the Lord there is mercy: and with him plentiful redemption.

8 And he shall redeem Israel from all his iniquities.

R. **With the Lord there is mercy and fullness of redemption.**

Living in the Spirit (Romans 8: 8-11):

8 And they who are in the flesh, cannot please God.

9 But you are not in the flesh, but in the spirit, if so be that the Spirit of God dwell in you. Now if any man

have not the Spirit of Christ, he is none of his.

10 And if Christ be in you, the body indeed is dead, because of sin; but the spirit liveth, because of justification.

11 And if the Spirit of him that raised up Jesus from the dead, dwell in you; he that raised up Jesus Christ from the dead, shall quicken also your mortal bodies, because of his Spirit that dwelleth in you.

The passage from Romans emphasizes the role of the Holy Spirit in our lives. Paul assures believers that those who belong to Christ have the Spirit living within them. The Spirit gives life to our mortal bodies, offering hope for the future.

Verse Before the Gospel: John 11: 25a, 26

25a, 26 I am the resurrection and the life, says the Lord; whoever believes in me, even if he dies, will never die.

The Raising of Lazarus (John 11: 1-45):

1 Now there was a certain man sick, named Lazarus, of Bethania, of the town of Mary and Martha her sister.

2 (And Mary was she that anointed the Lord with ointment, and wiped his feet with her hair: whose brother Lazarus was sick.)

3 His sisters therefore sent to him, saying: Lord, behold, he whom thou lovest is sick.

4 And Jesus hearing it, said to them: This sickness is not unto death, but for the glory of God: that the Son of God may be glorified by it.

5 Now Jesus loved Martha, and her sister Mary, and Lazarus.

6 When he had heard therefore that he was sick, he still remained in the same place two days.

7 Then after that, he said to his disciples: Let us go into Judea again.

8 The disciples say to him: Rabbi, the Jews but now sought to stone thee: and goest thou thither again?

9 Jesus answered: Are there not twelve hours of the day? If a man walk in the day, he stumbleth not, because he seeth the light of this world:

10 But if he walk in the night, he stumbleth, because the light is not in him.

11 These things he said; and after that he said to them: Lazarus our friend sleepeth; but I go that I may awake him out of sleep.

12 His disciples therefore said: Lord, if he sleep, he shall do well.

13 But Jesus spoke of his death; and they thought that he spoke of the repose of sleep.

14 Then therefore Jesus said to them plainly: Lazarus is dead.

15 And I am glad, for your sakes, that I was not there, that you may believe: but let us go to him.

16 Thomas therefore, who is called Didymus, said to his fellow disciples: Let us also go, that we may die with him.

17 Jesus therefore came, and found that he had been four days already in the grave.

18 (Now Bethania was near Jerusalem, about fifteen furlongs off.)

19 And many of the Jews were come to Martha and Mary, to comfort them concerning their brother.

20 Martha therefore, as soon as she heard that Jesus had come, went to meet him: but Mary sat at home.

21 Martha therefore said to Jesus: Lord, if thou hadst been here, my brother had not died.

22 But now also I know that whatsoever thou wilt ask of God, God will give it thee.

23 Jesus saith to her: Thy brother shall rise again.

24 Martha saith to him: I know that he shall rise again, in the resurrection at the last day.

25 Jesus said to her: I am the resurrection and the life: he that believeth in me, although he be dead, shall live:

26 And every one that liveth, and believeth in me, shall not die for ever. Believest thou this?

27 She saith to him: Yea, Lord, I have believed that thou art Christ the Son of the living God, who art come into this world.

28 And when she had said these things, she went, and called her sister Mary secretly, saying: The master is come, and calleth for thee.

29 She, as soon as she heard this, riseth quickly, and cometh to him.

30 For Jesus was not yet come into the town: but he was still in that place where Martha had met him.

31 The Jews therefore, who were with her in the house, and comforted her, when they saw Mary that she rose up speedily and went out, followed her, saying: She goeth to the grave to weep there.

32 When Mary therefore was come where Jesus was, seeing him, she fell down at his feet, and saith to him: Lord, if thou hadst been here, my brother had not died.

33 Jesus, therefore, when he saw her weeping, and the Jews that were come with her, weeping, groaned in the spirit, and troubled himself,

34 And said: Where have you laid him? They say to him: Lord, come and see.

35 And Jesus wept.

36 The Jews therefore said: Behold how he loved him.

37 But some of them said: Could not he that opened the eyes of the man born blind, have caused that this man should not die?

38 Jesus therefore again groaning in himself, cometh to the sepulchre. Now it was a cave; and a stone was laid over it.

39 Jesus saith: Take away the stone. Martha, the sister of him that was dead, saith to him: Lord, by this time he stinketh, for he is now of four days.

40 Jesus saith to her: Did not I say to thee, that if thou believe, thou shalt see the glory of God?

41 They took therefore the stone away. And Jesus lifting up his eyes said: Father, I give thee thanks that thou hast heard me.

42 And I knew that thou hearest me always; but because of the people who stand about have I said it, that they may believe that thou hast sent me.

43 When he had said these things, he cried with a loud voice: Lazarus, come forth.

44 And presently he that had been dead came forth, bound feet and hands with winding bands; and his face was bound about with a napkin. Jesus said to them: Loose him, and let him go.

45 Many therefore of the Jews, who were come to Mary and Martha, and had seen the things that Jesus did, believed in him.

The Gospel of John presents the remarkable story of Jesus

raising Lazarus from the dead. Lazarus, a friend of Jesus, has been dead for four days when Jesus arrives at his tomb. Despite the protests of those gathered, Jesus calls Lazarus out, and he emerges alive from the tomb. This event is a powerful demonstration of Jesus' authority over death and a foreshadowing of his own resurrection.

Reflect & Respond:

- How does the vision of the valley of dry bones in Ezekiel impact your understanding of God's power?

- Consider the concept of the Holy Spirit in Romans. How does the Holy Spirit bring life to your own life?

- The raising of Lazarus is a powerful story of hope. Has there ever been a time in your life when you felt hopeless? How can the story of Lazarus offer you comfort and hope?

Prayer:

Dear God, thank you for the gift of life and the promise of eternal hope. Grant us faith to believe in your power over death, even in the face of loss and grief. May the story of Lazarus remind us that you are the source of all life, and your love endures forever. Amen.

Challenge:

This week, spend some time reflecting on your own mortality. This doesn't have to be a morbid exercise, but rather an opportunity to appreciate the preciousness of life and the importance of living each day to the fullest. Consider reaching out to someone who is grieving or facing a difficult time. Your presence and compassion can be a source of comfort and hope.

Notes:_____

Sunday, April 13

- Passion (Palm) Sunday

Procession: Luke 19: 28-40

First Reading: Isaiah 50: 4-7

Responsorial Psalm: Psalms 22: 8-9, 17-18, 19-20, 23-24

Second Reading: Philippians 2:6-11

Verse Before the Gospel: Philippians 2: 8-9

Gospel: Luke 22: 14 - 23: 56

Lectionary: 37/38

Today marks Passion Sunday, also known as Palm Sunday, the beginning of Holy Week. The readings and traditions of this day set the stage for the dramatic events to unfold, culminating in the crucifixion and resurrection of Jesus Christ.

Processional with Palm Branches (Luke 19: 28-40):

28 And having said these things, he went before, going up to Jerusalem.

29 And it came to pass, when he was come nigh to Bethphage and Bethania, unto the mount called Olivet, he sent two of his disciples,

30 Saying: Go into the town which is over against you, at your entering into which you shall find the colt of an ass tied, on which no man ever hath sitten: loose him, and bring him hither.

31 And if any man shall ask you: Why do you loose him? you shall say thus unto him: Because the Lord hath need of his service.

32 And they that were sent, went their way, and found the colt standing, as he had said unto them.

33 And as they were loosing the colt, the owners thereof said to them: Why loose you the colt?

34 But they said: Because the Lord hath need of him.

35 And they brought him to Jesus. And casting their garments on the colt, they set Jesus thereon.

36 And as he went, they spread their clothes underneath in the way.

37 And when he was now coming near the descent of mount Olivet, the whole multitude of his disciples began with joy to praise God with a loud voice, for all the mighty works they had seen,

38 Saying: Blessed be the king who cometh in the name of the Lord, peace in heaven, and glory on high!

39 And some of the Pharisees, from amongst the multitude, said to him: Master, rebuke thy disciples.

40 To whom he said: I say to you, that if these shall hold their peace, the stones will cry out.

The day often begins with a processional, where participants wave palm branches, commemorating Jesus' triumphant entry into Jerusalem. The crowds hailed him as king, but this celebration would be short-lived.

The Suffering Servant (Isaiah 50: 4-7):

4 The Lord hath given me a learned tongue, that I should know how to uphold by word him that is weary: he wakeneth in the morning, in the morning he wakeneth my ear, that I may hear him as a master.

5 The Lord God hath opened my ear, and I do not resist: I have not gone back.

6 I have given my body to the strikers, and my cheeks to them that plucked them: I have not turned away my face from them that rebuked me, and spit upon me.

7 The Lord God is my helper, therefore am I not confounded: therefore have I set my face as a most hard rock, and I know that I shall not be confounded.

The first reading from Isaiah presents the concept of the suffering servant. This passage, written centuries before Jesus' arrival, foreshadows the Messiah's willingness to suffer and even die for his people.

R. (2a) My God, my God, why have you abandoned me?

8 All they that saw me have laughed me to scorn: they have spoken with the lips, and wagged the head.

9 He hoped in the Lord, let him deliver him: let him save him, seeing he delighteth in him.

R. My God, my God, why have you abandoned me?

17 For many dogs have encompassed me: the council of the malignant hath besieged me. They have dug my hands and feet.

18 They have numbered all my bones. And they have looked and stared upon me.

R. My God, my God, why have you abandoned me?

19 They parted my garments amongst them; and upon my vesture they cast lots.

20 But thou, O Lord, remove not thy help to a distance from me; look towards my defence.

R. My God, my God, why have you abandoned me?

23 I will declare thy name to my brethren: in the midst of the church will I praise thee.

24 Ye that fear the Lord, praise him: all ye the seed of Jacob, glorify him.

R. My God, my God, why have you abandoned me?

Humility and Obedience (Philippians 2: 6-11):

6 Who being in the form of God, thought it not robbery to be equal with God:

7 But emptied himself, taking the form of a servant, being made in the likeness of men, and in habit found as a man.

8 He humbled himself, becoming obedient unto death, even to the death of the cross.

9 For which cause God also hath exalted him, and hath given him a name which is above all names:

10 That in the name of Jesus every knee should bow, of those that are in heaven, on earth, and under the earth:

11 And that every tongue should confess that the Lord Jesus Christ is in the glory of God the Father.

The passage from Philippians emphasizes Jesus' humility and obedience. Though he was divine, Jesus emptied himself, taking the form of a servant and becoming obedient even to death on a cross. This act of selflessness serves as a model for Christian living.

Verse Before the Gospel: Philippians 2: 8-9

8-9 Christ became obedient to the point of death, even death on a cross. Because of this, God greatly exalted him and bestowed on him the name which is above every name.

The Passion Narrative (Luke 22: 14 - 23: 56):

14 And when the hour was come, he sat down, and the twelve apostles with him.

15 And he said to them: With desire I have desired to eat this pasch with you, before I suffer.

16 For I say to you, that from this time I will not eat it, till it be fulfilled in the kingdom of God.

17 And having taken the chalice, he gave thanks, and said: Take, and divide it among you:

18 For I say to you, that I will not drink of the fruit of the vine, till the kingdom of God come.

19 And taking bread, he gave thanks, and brake; and gave to them, saying: This is my body, which is given for you. Do this for a commemoration of me.

20 In like manner the chalice also, after he had supped, saying: This is the chalice, the new testament in my blood, which shall be shed for you.

21 But yet behold, the hand of him that betrayeth me is with me on the table.

22 And the Son of man indeed goeth, according to that which is determined: but yet, woe to that man by whom he shall be betrayed.

23 And they began to inquire among themselves, which of them it was that should do this thing.

24 And there was also a strife amongst them, which of them should seem to be the greater.

25 And he said to them: The kings of the Gentiles lord it over them; and they that have power over them, are called beneficent.

26 But you not so: but he that is the greater among you, let him become as the younger; and he that is the leader, as he that serveth.

27 For which is greater, he that sitteth at table, or he that serveth? Is it not he that sitteth at table? But I am in the midst of you, as he that serveth:

28 And you are they who have continued with me in my temptations:

29 And I dispose to you, as my Father hath disposed to me, a kingdom;

30 That you may eat and drink at my table, in my kingdom: and may sit upon thrones, judging the twelve tribes of Israel.

31 And the Lord said: Simon, Simon, behold Satan hath desired to have you, that he may sift you as wheat:

32 But I have prayed for thee, that thy faith fail not: and thou, being once converted, confirm thy brethren.

33 Who said to him: Lord, I am ready to go with thee, both into prison, and to death.

34 And he said: I say to thee, Peter, the cock shall not crow this day, till thou thrice deniest that thou knowest me. And he said to them:

35 When I sent you without purse, and scrip, and shoes, did you want anything?

36 But they said: Nothing. Then said he unto them: But now he that hath a purse, let him take it, and likewise a scrip; and he that hath not, let him sell his coat, and buy a sword.

37 For I say to you, that this that is written must yet be fulfilled in me: And with the wicked was he reckoned. For the things concerning me have an end.

38 But they said: Lord, behold here are two swords. And he said to them, It is enough.

39 And going out, he went, according to his custom, to the mount of

Olives. And his disciples also followed him.

40 And when he was come to the place, he said to them: Pray, lest ye enter into temptation.

41 And he was withdrawn away from them a stone's cast; and kneeling down, he prayed,

42 Saying: Father, if thou wilt, remove this chalice from me: but yet not my will, but thine be done.

43 And there appeared to him an angel from heaven, strengthening him. And being in an agony, he prayed the longer.

44 And his sweat became as drops of blood, trickling down upon the ground.

45 And when he rose up from prayer, and was come to his disciples, he found them sleeping for sorrow.

46 And he said to them: Why sleep you? arise, pray, lest you enter into temptation.

47 As he was yet speaking, behold a multitude; and he that was called Judas, one of the twelve, went before them, and drew near to Jesus, for to kiss him.

48 And Jesus said to him: Judas, dost thou betray the Son of man with a kiss?

49 And they that were about him, seeing what would follow, said to him: Lord, shall we strike with the sword?

50 And one of them struck the servant of the high priest, and cut off his right ear.

51 But Jesus answering, said: Suffer ye thus far. And when he had touched his ear, he healed him.

52 And Jesus said to the chief priests, and magistrates of the temple, and the ancients, that were come unto him: Are ye come out, as it were against a thief, with swords and clubs?

53 When I was daily with you in the temple, you did not stretch forth your hands against me: but this is your hour, and the power of darkness.

54 And apprehending him, they led him to the high priest's house. But Peter followed afar off.

55 And when they had kindled a fire in the midst of the hall, and were sitting about it, Peter was in the midst of them.

56 Whom when a certain servant maid had seen sitting at the light, and had earnestly beheld him, she said: This man also was with him.

57 But he denied him, saying: Woman, I know him not.

58 And after a little while, another seeing him, said: Thou also art one of them. But Peter said: O man, I am not.

59 And after the space, as it were of one hour, another certain man affirmed, saying: Of a truth, this man was also with him; for he is also a Galilean.

60 And Peter said: Man, I know not what thou sayest. And immediately, as he was yet speaking, the cock crew.

61 And the Lord turning looked on Peter. And Peter remembered the word of the Lord, as he had said: Before the cock crow, thou shalt deny me thrice.

62 And Peter going out, wept bitterly.

63 And the men that held him, mocked him, and struck him.

64 And they blindfolded him, and smote his face. And they asked him, saying: Prophesy, who is it that struck thee?

65 And blaspheming, many other things they said against him.

66 And as soon as it was day, the ancients of the people, and the chief priests and scribes, came together; and they brought him into their council, saying: If thou be the Christ, tell us.

67 And he saith to them: If I shall tell you, you will not believe me.

68 And if I shall also ask you, you will not answer me, nor let me go.

69 But hereafter the Son of man shall be sitting on the right hand of the power of God.

70 Then said they all: Art thou then the Son of God? Who said: You say that I am.

71 And they said: What need we any further testimony? for we ourselves have heard it from his own mouth.

23:1 And the whole multitude of them rising up, led him to Pilate.

2 And they began to accuse him, saying: We have found this man perverting our nation, and forbidding to give tribute to Caesar, and saying that he is Christ the king.

3 And Pilate asked him, saying: Art thou the king of the Jews? But he answering, said: Thou sayest it.

4 And Pilate said to the chief priests and to the multitudes: I find no cause in this man.

5 But they were more earnest, saying: He stirreth up the people, teaching throughout all Judea, beginning from Galilee to this place.

6 But Pilate hearing Galilee, asked if the man were of Galilee?

7 And when he understood that he was of Herod's jurisdiction, he sent him away to Herod, who was also himself at Jerusalem, in those days.

8 And Herod, seeing Jesus, was very glad; for he was desirous of a long time to see him, because he had heard many things of him; and he hoped to see some sign wrought by him.

9 And he questioned him in many words. But he answered him nothing.

10 And the chief priests and the scribes stood by, earnestly accusing him.

11 And Herod with his army set him at nought, and mocked him, putting on him a white garment, and sent him back to Pilate.

12 And Herod and Pilate were made friends, that same day; for before they were enemies one to another.

13 And Pilate, calling together the chief priests, and the magistrates, and the people,

14 Said to them: You have presented unto me this man, as one that perverteth the people; and behold I, having examined him before you, find no cause in this man, in those things wherein you accuse him.

15 No, nor Herod neither. For I sent you to him, and behold, nothing worthy of death is done to him.

16 I will chastise him therefore, and release him.

17 Now of necessity he was to release unto them one upon the feast day.

18 But the whole multitude together cried out, saying: Away with this man, and release unto us Barabbas:

19 Who, for a certain sedition made in the city, and for a murder, was cast into prison.

20 And Pilate again spoke to them, desiring to release Jesus.

21 But they cried again, saying: Crucify him, crucify him.

22 And he said to them the third time: Why, what evil hath this man done? I find no cause of death in him. I will chastise him therefore, and let him go.

23 But they were instant with loud voices, requiring that he might be crucified; and their voices prevailed.

24 And Pilate gave sentence that it should be as they required.

25 And he released unto them him who for murder and sedition, had been cast into prison, whom they had desired; but Jesus he delivered up to their will.

26 And as they led him away, they laid hold of one Simon of Cyrene, coming from the country; and they laid the cross on him to carry after Jesus.

27 And there followed him a great multitude of people, and of women, who bewailed and lamented him.

28 But Jesus turning to them, said: Daughters of Jerusalem, weep not over me; but weep for yourselves, and for your children.

29 For behold, the days shall come, wherein they will say: Blessed are the barren, and the wombs that have not borne, and the paps that have not given suck.

30 Then shall they begin to say to the mountains: Fall upon us; and to the hills: Cover us.

31 For if in the green wood they do these things, what shall be done in the dry?

32 And there were also two other malefactors led with him to be put to death.

33 And when they were come to the place which is called Calvary, they crucified him there; and the robbers, one on the right hand, and the other on the left.

34 And Jesus said: Father, forgive them, for they know not what they do. But they, dividing his garments, cast lots.

35 And the people stood beholding, and the rulers with them derided him, saying: He saved others; let him save himself, if he be Christ, the elect of God.

36 And the soldiers also mocked him, coming to him, and offering him vinegar,

37 And saying: If thou be the king of the Jews, save thyself.

38 And there was also a superscription written over him in letters of Greek, and Latin, and Hebrew: THIS IS THE KING OF THE JEWS.

39 And one of those robbers who were hanged, blasphemed him, saying: If thou be Christ, save thyself and us.

40 But the other answering, rebuked him, saying: Neither dost thou fear God, seeing thou art condemned under the same condemnation?

41 And we indeed justly, for we receive the due reward of our deeds; but this man hath done no evil.

42 And he said to Jesus: Lord, remember me when thou shalt come into thy kingdom.

43 And Jesus said to him: Amen I say to thee, this day thou shalt be with me in paradise.

44 And it was almost the sixth hour; and there was darkness over all the earth until the ninth hour.

45 And the sun was darkened, and the veil of the temple was rent in the midst.

46 And Jesus crying out with a loud voice, said: Father, into thy hands I commend my spirit. And saying this, he gave up the ghost.

47 Now the centurion, seeing what was done, glorified God, saying: Indeed this was a just man.

48 And all the multitude of them that were come together to that sight, and saw the things that were done, returned striking their breasts.

49 And all his acquaintance, and the women that had followed him from Galilee, stood afar off, beholding these things.

50 And behold there was a man named Joseph, who was a counsellor, a good and just man,

51 (The same had not consented to their counsel and doings;) of Arimathea, a city of Judea; who also himself looked for the kingdom of God.

52 This man went to Pilate, and begged the body of Jesus.

53 And taking him down, he wrapped him in fine linen, and laid him in a sepulchre that was hewed in stone, wherein never yet any man had been laid.

54 And it was the day of the Parasceve, and the sabbath drew on.

55 And the women that were come with him from Galilee, following after, saw the sepulchre, and how his body was laid.

56 And returning, they prepared spices and ointments; and on the sabbath day they rested, according to the commandment.

The Gospel of Luke presents a detailed account of Jesus' passion, his suffering and death on the cross. This lengthy passage recounts the Last Supper, Jesus' betrayal by Judas, his arrest, trial, crucifixion, and burial.

Reflect & Respond:

- How do the traditions of Palm Sunday, such as the processional with palm branches, help you enter into the spirit of Holy Week?

- Consider the concept of the suffering servant in Isaiah. How does this idea challenge your understanding of power and leadership?

- Jesus' humility and obedience are central themes in Philippians. Are there areas in your own life where you need to practice more humility or obedience?

- The Passion narrative is a powerful story of sacrifice and love. How does this story impact your understanding of Jesus' mission and message?

Prayer:

Dear God, as we enter Holy Week, help us to contemplate the profound significance of Jesus' sacrifice. Grant us the courage to face our own challenges with faith and humility. May your love and compassion guide us through this sacred time of reflection and remembrance. Amen.

Challenge:

This week, set aside some time each day for quiet reflection or prayer. Consider reading through the Passion narratives in the other Gospels (Matthew, Mark, and John) to gain a more comprehensive understanding of Jesus' final days. Holy Week is a time for contemplating the depths of Jesus' love and sacrifice.

Notes:_____

_____
_____
_____
_____
_____
_____
_____
_____
_____
_____
_____
_____
_____
_____
_____
_____
_____
_____
_____
_____
_____
_____
_____

_____
_____
_____
_____
_____
_____
_____
_____
_____
_____
_____
_____
_____
_____
_____
_____
_____
_____
_____
_____
_____
_____
_____
_____
_____
_____
_____
_____
_____
_____

Sunday, April 20

- Easter Sunday - Solemnity

First Reading: Acts 10: 34a, 37-43

Responsorial Psalm: Psalms 118: 1-2, 16-17, 22-23

Second Reading: Colossians 3: 1-4 or First Corinthians 5: 6b-8

Alleluia: First Corinthians 5: 7b-8a

Gospel: John 20: 1-9 or Matthew 28: 1-10 or, at an afternoon or evening Mass, Luke 24: 13-35

Lectionary: 42

Hallelujah! Easter Sunday, the culmination of Holy Week, is the most joyous and important celebration in Christianity. It marks the resurrection of Jesus Christ from the dead, signifying victory over death and the promise of eternal life.

The Good News of the Resurrection (Acts 10: 34a, 37-43):

34a And Peter opening his mouth, said:

37 You know the word which hath been published through all Judea: for it began from Galilee, after the baptism which John preached,

38 Jesus of Nazareth: how God anointed him with the Holy Ghost, and with power, who went about doing good, and healing all that were oppressed by the devil, for God was with him.

39 And we are witnesses of all things that he did in the land of the Jews and in Jerusalem, whom they killed, hanging him upon a tree.

40 Him God raised up the third day, and gave him to be made manifest,

41 Not to all the people, but to witnesses preordained by God, even to us, who did eat and drink with him after he arose again from the dead;

42 And he commanded us to preach to the people, and to testify that it is he who was appointed by God, to be judge of the living and of the dead.

43 To him all the prophets give testimony, that by his name all receive remission of sins, who believe in him.

The first reading from Acts recounts Peter's sermon to Cornelius, a Roman centurion. Peter proclaims the good news of Jesus' resurrection, emphasizing that it was witnessed by many. This event is the cornerstone of the Christian faith.

Responsorial Psalm: Psalms 118: 1-2, 16-17, 22-23

R. (24) This is the day the Lord has made; let us rejoice and be glad.

Or R. Alleluia.

1 Give praise to Lord, for he is good: for his mercy endureth for ever.

2 Let Israel now say that he is good: that his mercy endureth for ever.

R. This is the day the Lord has made; let us rejoice and be glad.

Or R. Alleluia.

16 The right hand of the Lord hath wrought strength: the right hand of the Lord hath exulted me: the right hand of the Lord hath wrought strength.

17 I shall not die, but live: and shall declare the works of the Lord.

R. This is the day the Lord has made; let us rejoice and be glad.

Or R. Alleluia.

22 The stone which the builders rejected; the same is become the head of the corner.

23 This is the Lord's doing: and it is wonderful in our eyes.

R. This is the day the Lord has made; let us rejoice and be glad.

Or R. Alleluia.

New Life in Christ (Colossians 3: 1-4 or 1 Corinthians 5: 6b-8):

1 Therefore, if you be risen with Christ, seek the things that are above; where Christ is sitting at the right hand of God:

2 Mind the things that are above, not the things that are upon the earth.

3 For you are dead; and your life is hid with Christ in God.

4 When Christ shall appear, who is your life, then you also shall appear with him in glory.

Or

6b Know you not that a little leaven corrupteth the whole lump?

7 Purge out the old leaven, that you may be a new paste, as you are unleavened. For Christ our pasch is sacrificed.

8 Therefore let us feast, not with the old leaven, nor with the leaven of malice and wickedness; but with the unleavened bread of sincerity and truth.

The second reading offers a message of hope and transformation. Colossians emphasizes that if we have been raised with Christ, we should seek the things that are above, where Christ is seated at the right hand of God. 1 Corinthians uses the analogy of removing old leaven to represent putting away sin and celebrating the festival of the new life we have in Christ.

Alleluia: First Corinthians 5: 7b-8a

R. Alleluia, alleluia.

7b-8a Christ, our paschal lamb, has been sacrificed; let us then feast with joy in the Lord.

R. Alleluia, alleluia.

The Empty Tomb (John 20: 1-9 or Matthew 28: 1-10 or Luke 24: 13-35):

1 And on the first day of the week, Mary Magdalen cometh early, when it was yet dark, unto the sepulchre; and she saw the stone taken away from the sepulchre.

2 She ran, therefore, and cometh to Simon Peter, and to the other disciple whom Jesus loved, and saith to them: They have taken away the Lord out of the sepulchre, and we know not where they have laid him.

3 Peter therefore went out, and that other disciple, and they came to the sepulchre.

4 And they both ran together, and that other disciple did outrun Peter, and came first to the sepulchre.

5 And when he stooped down, he saw the linen cloths lying: but yet he went not in.

6 Then cometh Simon Peter, following him, and went into the sepulchre, and saw the linen cloths lying,

7 And the napkin that had been about his head, not lying with the linen cloths, but apart, wrapped up into one place.

8 Then that other disciple also went in, who came first to the sepulchre: and he saw, and believed.

9 For as yet they knew not the scripture, that he must rise again from the dead.

Or

1 And in the end of the sabbath, when it began to dawn towards the first day of the week, came Mary Magdalen and the other Mary, to see the sepulchre.

2 And behold there was a great earthquake. For an angel of the Lord descended from heaven, and coming, rolled back the stone, and sat upon it.

3 And his countenance was as lightning, and his raiment as snow.

4 And for fear of him, the guards were struck with terror, and became as dead men.

5 And the angel answering, said to the women: Fear not you: for I know that you seek Jesus who was crucified.

6 He is not here, for he is risen, as he said. Come, and see the place where the Lord was laid.

7 And going quickly, tell ye his disciples that he is risen: and behold he will go before you into Galilee; there you shall see him. Lo, I have foretold it to you.

8 And they went out quickly from the sepulchre with fear and great joy, running to tell his disciples.

9 And behold Jesus met them, saying: All hail. But they came up and took hold of his feet, and adored him.

10 Then Jesus said to them: Fear not. Go, tell my brethren that they go into Galilee, there they shall see me.

Or at an afternoon or evening Mass

13 And behold, two of them went, the same day, to a town which was sixty furlongs from Jerusalem, named Emmaus.

14 And they talked together of all these things which had happened.

15 And it came to pass, that while they talked and reasoned with themselves, Jesus himself also drawing near, went with them.

16 But their eyes were held, that they should not know him.

17 And he said to them: What are these discourses that you hold one with another as you walk, and are sad?

18 And the one of them, whose name was Cleophas, answering, said to him: Art thou only a stranger to Jerusalem, and hast not known the things that have been done there in these days?

19 To whom he said: What things? And they said: Concerning Jesus of Nazareth, who was a prophet, mighty in work and word before God and all the people;

20 And how our chief priests and princes delivered him to be condemned to death, and crucified him.

21 But we hoped, that it was he that should have redeemed Israel: and now besides all this, today is the third day since these things were done.

22 Yea and certain women also of our company affrighted us, who before it was light, were at the sepulchre,

23 And not finding his body, came, saying, that they had also seen a vision of angels, who say that he is alive.

24 And some of our people went to the sepulchre, and found it so as the women had said, but him they found not.

25 Then he said to them: O foolish, and slow of heart to believe in all things which the prophets have spoken.

26 Ought not Christ to have suffered these things, and so to enter into his glory?

27 And beginning at Moses and all the prophets, he expounded to them in all the scriptures, the things that were concerning him.

28 And they drew nigh to the town, whither they were going: and he made as though he would go farther.

29 But they constrained him; saying: Stay with us, because it is towards evening, and the day is now far spent. And he went in with them.

30 And it came to pass, whilst he was at table with them, he took bread, and blessed, and brake, and gave to them.

31 And their eyes were opened, and they knew him: and he vanished out of their sight.

32 And they said one to the other: Was not our heart burning within us, whilst he spoke in this way, and opened to us the scriptures?

33 And rising up, the same hour, they went back to Jerusalem: and they found the eleven gathered together, and those that were staying with them,

34 Saying: The Lord is risen indeed, and hath appeared to Simon.

35 And they told what things were done in the way; and how they knew him in the breaking of the bread.

The Gospel reading recounts the discovery of the empty tomb. Depending on the specific Gospel chosen, details may vary, but the core message remains the same: Jesus is no longer dead, he has risen! This event filled the disciples with joy and hope, and it continues to be a source of inspiration for Christians today.

Reflect & Respond:

- How does the celebration of Easter Sunday fill you with joy and hope?

- Consider the concept of new life in Christ. How does this concept impact the way you live your life?

- The empty tomb is a powerful symbol of Jesus' resurrection. What does this symbol mean to you?

Prayer:

Dear God, we rejoice in the glorious resurrection of your Son, Jesus Christ. Your victory over death fills us with hope and grants us new life. May we share the good news of your love with the world and live according to the teachings of your risen Son. Amen.

Challenge:

This Easter season, let the joy of the resurrection spill over into your interactions with others. Spread kindness and compassion, and be a source of light and hope in the world. Remember, the Easter message is one of new beginnings, so embrace opportunities for growth and transformation in your own life.

Notes:_____

_____

_____

_____

_____

Sunday, April 27

- Second Sunday of Easter

First Reading: Acts 5: 12-16

Responsorial Psalm: Psalms 118: 2-4, 13-15, 22-24

Second Reading: Revelation 1: 9-11a, 12-13, 17-19

Alleluia: John 20: 29

Gospel: John 20:19-31

Lectionary: 45

This Second Sunday of Easter, also known as Divine Mercy Sunday, focuses on God's boundless mercy and forgiveness. The readings highlight the importance of faith and the transforming power of encountering the risen Christ.

The Early Church in Jerusalem (Acts 5: 12-16):

12 And by the hands of the apostles were many signs and wonders wrought among the people. And they were all with one accord in Solomon's porch.

13 But of the rest no man durst join himself unto them; but the people magnified them.

14 And the multitude of men and women who believed in the Lord, was more increased:

15 Insomuch that they brought forth the sick into the streets, and laid them on beds and couches, that when Peter came, his shadow at the least, might overshadow any of them, and they might be delivered from their infirmities.

16 And there came also together to Jerusalem a multitude out of the neighbouring cities, bringing sick persons, and such as were troubled with unclean spirits; who were all healed.

The first reading from Acts recounts the growth of the early church in Jerusalem. The apostles perform many signs and wonders, and the people hold them in high regard. This passage serves as a reminder of the power of the Holy Spirit working through the early believers.

Responsorial Psalm: Psalms 118: 2-4, 13-15, 22-24

R. (1) Give thanks to the Lord for he is good, his love is everlasting.
Or R. Alleluia.
2 Let Israel now say that he is good: that his mercy endureth for ever.
3 Let the house of Aaron now say, that his mercy endureth for ever.
4 Let them that fear the Lord now say, that his mercy endureth for ever.
R. Give thanks to the Lord for he is good, his love is everlasting.
Or R. Alleluia.
13 Being pushed I was overturned that I might fall: but the Lord supported me.
14 The Lord is my strength and my praise: and he is become my salvation.

15 The voice of rejoicing and of salvation is in the tabernacles of the just.
R. Give thanks to the Lord for he is good, his love is everlasting.
Or R. Alleluia.
22 The stone which the builders rejected; the same is become the head of the corner.
23 This is the Lord's doing: and it is wonderful in our eyes.
24 This is the day which the Lord hath made: let us be glad and rejoice therein.
R. Give thanks to the Lord for he is good, his love is everlasting.
Or R. Alleluia.

The Vision of Patmos (Revelation 1: 9-11a, 12-13, 17-19):

9 I John, your brother and your partner in tribulation, and in the kingdom, and patience in Christ Jesus, was in the island, which is called Patmos, for the word of God, and for the testimony of Jesus.

10 I was in the spirit on the Lord's day, and heard behind me a great voice, as of a trumpet,

11a Saying: What thou seest, write in a book.

12 And I turned to see the voice that spoke with me. And being turned, I saw seven golden candlesticks:

13 And in the midst of the seven golden candlesticks, one like to the Son of man, clothed with a garment down to the feet, and girt about the paps with a golden girdle.

17 And when I had seen him, I fell at his feet as dead. And he laid his right hand upon me, saying: Fear not. I am the First and the Last,

18 And alive, and was dead, and behold I am living for ever and ever, and have the keys of death and of hell.

19 Write therefore the things which thou hast seen, and which are, and which must be done hereafter.

The second reading presents a glimpse of the book of Revelation. The author, John, describes being exiled on the island of Patmos, where he receives a vision of the risen Christ. This encounter fills John with awe and empowers him to share the message of God's revelation.

Alleluia: John 20: 29

R. Alleluia, alleluia.

29 You believe in me, Thomas, because you have seen me, says the Lord; blessed are those who have not seen me, but still believe!

R. Alleluia, alleluia.

Encountering the Risen Christ (John 20:19-31):

19 Now when it was late that same day, the first of the week, and the doors were shut, where the disciples were gathered together, for fear of the Jews, Jesus came and stood in the midst, and said to them: Peace be to you.

20 And when he had said this, he shewed them his hands and his side. The disciples therefore were glad, when they saw the Lord.

21 He said therefore to them again: Peace be to you. As the Father hath sent me, I also send you.

22 When he had said this, he breathed on them; and he said to them: Receive ye the Holy Ghost.

23 Whose sins you shall forgive, they are forgiven them; and whose sins you shall retain, they are retained.

24 Now Thomas, one of the twelve, who is called Didymus, was not with them when Jesus came.

25 The other disciples therefore said to him: We have seen the Lord. But he said to them: Except I shall see in his hands the print of the nails, and put my finger into the place of the nails, and put my hand into his side, I will not believe.

26 And after eight days again his disciples were within, and Thomas with them. Jesus cometh, the doors being shut, and stood in the midst, and said: Peace be to you.

27 Then he saith to Thomas: Put in thy finger hither, and see my hands; and bring hither thy hand, and put it into my side; and be not faithless, but believing.

28 Thomas answered, and said to him: My Lord, and my God.

29 Jesus saith to him: Because thou hast seen me, Thomas, thou hast believed: blessed are they that have not seen, and have believed.

30 Many other signs also did Jesus in the sight of his disciples, which are not written in this book.

31 But these are written, that you may believe that Jesus is the Christ, the Son of God: and that believing, you may have life in his name.

The Gospel of John presents the story of Jesus appearing to his disciples after the resurrection, eight days after the first Easter Sunday. Thomas, also known as "doubting Thomas," is not present at this initial appearance. When he hears the news from the other disciples, he expresses skepticism. A week later, Jesus appears again to the disciples, and this time Thomas is present. Jesus invites Thomas to touch his wounds, and Thomas finally believes, proclaiming, "My Lord and my God!" This story emphasizes the importance of faith, but also the openness of Jesus to those who doubt.

Reflect & Respond:

- How does the story of the early church in Acts inspire you to share your faith with others?

- Consider the concept of divine mercy. Have you experienced God's mercy in your own life? How can you be a channel of God's mercy to others?

- The story of doubting Thomas reminds us that faith can grow even amidst doubt. Have you ever struggled with doubt? How can you strengthen your faith?

Prayer:

Dear God, we praise you for your boundless mercy and love. Thank you for the gift of faith and the opportunity to encounter you, the risen Christ. Grant us the courage to share your message of hope with the world and to be instruments of your mercy in all that we do. Amen.

Challenge:

This week, practice a random act of kindness or forgiveness. This could be anything from offering to help someone in need to letting go of a grudge you've been holding onto. By extending mercy to others, we reflect the divine mercy that God so generously pours out on us.

Notes:_____

_____

_____

_____

_____

_____

_____

_____

_____

_____

_____

_____

_____

May 2025

Sunday, May 4

- Third Sunday of Easter

First Reading: Acts 5: 27-32, 40b-41

Responsorial Psalm: Psalms 30: 2 and 4, 5-6, 11-12, 13

Second Reading: Revelation 5: 11-14

Gospel: John 21: 1-19

Lectionary: 48

This Third Sunday of Easter invites us to reflect on the call to follow Jesus, the Good Shepherd, who guides, protects, and cares for his flock. The readings emphasize the importance of faith, perseverance, and service in the Christian life.

The Apostles on Trial (Acts 5: 27-32, 40b-41):

27 And when they had brought them, they set them before the council. And the high priest asked them,

28 Saying: Commanding we commanded you, that you should not teach in this name; and behold, you have filled Jerusalem with your doctrine, and you have a mind to bring the blood of this man upon us.

29 But Peter and the apostles answering, said: We ought to obey God, rather than men.

30 The God of our fathers hath raised up Jesus, whom you put to death, hanging him upon a tree.

31 Him hath God exalted with his right hand, to be Prince and Saviour, to give repentance to Israel, and remission of sins.

32 And we are witnesses of these things and the Holy Ghost, whom God hath given to all that obey him.

40b They charged them that they should not speak at all in the name of Jesus; and they dismissed them.

41 And they indeed went from the presence of the council, rejoicing that they were accounted worthy to

suffer reproach for the name of Jesus.

The first reading from Acts picks up on the story of the early church. The apostles are brought before the authorities for preaching about Jesus. They remain faithful to their message, even in the face of threats. This passage highlights the courage and perseverance of the early Christians.

Responsorial Psalm: Psalms 30: 2 and 4, 5-6, 11-12, 13

R. (2a) I will praise you, Lord, for you have rescued me.
or
R. Alleluia.
2 I will extol thee, O Lord, for thou hast upheld me: and hast not made my enemies to rejoice over me.
4 Thou hast brought forth, O Lord, my soul from hell: thou hast saved me from them that go down into the pit.
R. I will praise you, Lord, for you have rescued me.
or

R. Alleluia.
5 Sing to the Lord, O ye his saints: and give praise to the memory of his holiness.
6 For wrath is in his indignation; and life in his good will. In the evening weeping shall have place, and in the morning gladness.
R. I will praise you, Lord, for you have rescued me.
or
R. Alleluia.
11 The Lord hath heard, and hath had mercy on me: the Lord became my helper.
12 Thou hast turned for me my mourning into joy: thou hast cut my sackcloth, and hast compassed me with gladness:
R. I will praise you, Lord, for you have rescued me.
or
R. Alleluia.
13 To the end that my glory may sing to thee, and I may not regret: O Lord my God, I will give praise to thee for ever.
R. I will praise you, Lord, for you have rescued me.
or
R. Alleluia.

The Worthy Lamb (Revelation 5: 11-14):

11 And I beheld, and I heard the voice of many angels round about the throne, and the living creatures, and the ancients; and the number of them was thousands of thousands,

12 Saying with a loud voice: The Lamb that was slain is worthy to receive power, and divinity, and wisdom, and strength, and honour, and glory, and benediction.

13 And every creature, which is in heaven, and on the earth, and under the earth, and such as are in the sea, and all that are in them: I heard all saying: To him that sitteth on the throne, and to the Lamb, benediction, and honour, and glory, and power, for ever and ever.

14 And the four living creatures said: Amen. And the four and twenty ancients fell down on their faces, and adored him that liveth for ever and ever.

The second reading from Revelation presents a beautiful image of the Lamb, worthy to take the scroll and open its seals. This Lamb is a symbol of Jesus Christ, who is victorious over sin and death. The passage emphasizes his worthiness to receive worship and praise.

Alleluia

R. Alleluia, alleluia.

Christ is risen, creator of all; he has shown pity on all people.

R. Alleluia, alleluia.

The Restoration of Peter (John 21: 1-19):

1 After this, Jesus shewed himself again to the disciples at the sea of Tiberias. And he shewed himself after this manner.

2 There were together Simon Peter, and Thomas, who is called Didymus, and Nathanael, who was of Cana of Galilee, and the sons of Zebedee, and two others of his disciples.

3 Simon Peter saith to them: I go a fishing. They say to him: We also come with thee. And they went forth, and entered into the ship: and that night they caught nothing.

4 But when the morning was come, Jesus stood on the shore: yet the disciples knew not that it was Jesus.

5 Jesus therefore said to them: Children, have you any meat? They answered him: No.

6 He saith to them: Cast the net on the right side of the ship, and you shall find. They cast therefore; and now they were not able to draw it, for the multitude of fishes.

7 That disciple therefore whom Jesus loved, said to Peter: It is the Lord. Simon Peter, when he heard that it was the Lord, girt his coat about him, (for he was naked,) and cast himself into the sea.

8 But the other disciples came in the ship, (for they were not far from the land, but as it were two hundred cubits,) dragging the net with fishes.

9 As soon then as they came to land, they saw hot coals lying, and a fish laid thereon, and bread.

10 Jesus saith to them: Bring hither of the fishes which you have now caught.

11 Simon Peter went up, and drew the net to land, full of great fishes, one hundred and fifty-three. And although there were so many, the net was not broken.

12 Jesus saith to them: Come, and dine. And none of them who were at meat, durst ask him: Who art thou? knowing that it was the Lord.

13 And Jesus cometh and taketh bread, and giveth them, and fish in like manner.

14 This is now the third time that Jesus was manifested to his disciples, after he was risen from the dead.

15 When therefore they had dined, Jesus saith to Simon Peter: Simon son of John, lovest thou me more than these? He saith to him: Yea, Lord, thou knowest that I love thee. He saith to him: Feed my lambs.

16 He saith to him again: Simon, son of John, lovest thou me? He saith to him: Yea, Lord, thou knowest that I love thee. He saith to him: Feed my lambs.

17 He said to him the third time: Simon, son of John, lovest thou me? Peter was grieved, because he had said to him the third time: Lovest thou me? And he said to him: Lord, thou knowest all things: thou knowest that I love thee. He said to him: Feed my sheep.

18 Amen, amen I say to thee, when thou wast younger, thou didst gird thyself, and didst walk where thou wouldst. But when thou shalt be old, thou shalt stretch forth thy hands, and another shall gird thee, and lead thee whither thou wouldst not.

19 And this he said, signifying by what death he should glorify God. And when he had said this, he saith to him: Follow me.

The Gospel of John recounts the story of Jesus appearing to his disciples at the Sea of Galilee. Peter, who had previously denied Jesus three times, is given the opportunity to reaffirm his love and devotion. Jesus entrusts Peter with the task of feeding his sheep, symbolizing Peter's role as a shepherd within the church. This passage highlights God's forgiveness and his willingness to restore those who have fallen.

Reflect & Respond:

- How does the story of the apostles in Acts inspire you to be courageous in your faith?

- Consider the concept of Jesus as the Lamb in Revelation. How does this image impact your understanding of Jesus' sacrifice?

- The restoration of Peter is a powerful story of forgiveness and new beginnings. Is there a relationship in your life that needs mending? How can you take steps towards reconciliation?

Prayer:

Dear God, thank you for your love and guidance. Help us to follow you, the Good Shepherd, with faith and obedience. Grant us the courage to share your message with the world and to serve others with love and compassion. May we be instruments of your peace and healing in all that we do. Amen.

Challenge:

This week, consider your own gifts and talents. How can you

use them to serve others and build up the body of Christ, the church? Look for opportunities to volunteer your time or share your skills with those in need. Remember, even small acts of service can make a big difference.

Notes:_____

_____
_____
_____
_____
_____
_____
_____
_____
_____
_____
_____
_____
_____
_____
_____
_____
_____
_____
_____

_____
_____
_____
_____
_____
_____
_____
_____
_____
_____
_____
_____
_____
_____
_____
_____
_____
_____
_____
_____
_____
_____
_____
_____
_____
_____
_____
_____
_____

Sunday, May 11

- Fourth Sunday of Easter

First Reading: Acts 13: 14, 43-52

Responsorial Psalm: Psalms 100: 1-2, 3, 5

Second Reading: Revelation 7: 9, 14b-17

Alleluia: John 10: 14

Gospel: John 10: 27-30

Lectionary: 51

This Fourth Sunday of Easter invites us to reflect on the relationship between Jesus, the Good Shepherd, and his flock, the believers. The readings emphasize the themes of belonging, protection, and the enduring love between Jesus and his followers.

Paul and Barnabas in Antioch (Acts 13: 14, 43-52):

14 But they passing through Perge, came to Antioch in Pisidia: and entering into the synagogue on the sabbath day, they sat down.

43 And when the synagogue was broken up, many of the Jews, and of the strangers who served God, followed Paul and Barnabas: who speaking to them, persuaded them to continue in the grace of God.

44 But the next sabbath day, the whole city almost came together, to hear the word of God.

45 And the Jews seeing the multitudes, were filled with envy, and contradicted those things which were said by Paul, blaspheming.

46 Then Paul and Barnabas said boldly: To you it behoved us first to speak the word of God: but because you reject it, and judge yourselves unworthy of eternal life, behold we turn to the Gentiles.

47 For so the Lord hath commanded us: I have set thee to be the light of the Gentiles; that thou mayest be for salvation unto the utmost part of the earth.

48 And the Gentiles hearing it, were glad, and glorified the word of the Lord: and as many as were ordained to life everlasting, believed.

49 And the word of the Lord was published throughout the whole country.

50 But the Jews stirred up religious and honourable women, and the chief men of the city, and raised persecution against Paul and Barnabas: and cast them out of their coasts.

51 But they, shaking off the dust of their feet against them, came to Iconium.

52 And the disciples were filled with joy and with the Holy Ghost.

The first reading from Acts recounts the missionary journey of Paul and Barnabas. They arrive in Antioch and begin preaching the gospel to both Jews and Gentiles. Many people respond positively to their message, and a large number of disciples are formed. This passage highlights the spread of Christianity beyond the Jewish community.

Responsorial Psalm: Psalms 100: 1-2, 3, 5

R. (3c) We are his people, the sheep of his flock.
or
R. Alleluia.
1-2 Sing joyfully to God, all the earth: serve ye the Lord with gladness. Come in before his presence with exceeding great joy.
R. We are his people, the sheep of his flock.
or
R. Alleluia.
3 Know ye that the Lord he is God: he made us, and not we ourselves. We are his people and the sheep of his pasture.
R. We are his people, the sheep of his flock.
or
R. Alleluia.
5 For the Lord is sweet, his mercy endureth for ever, and his truth to generation and generation.
R. We are his people, the sheep of his flock.
or
R. Alleluia.

The Great Multitude in White Robes (Revelation 7: 9, 14b-17):

9 After this I saw a great multitude, which no man could number, of all nations, and tribes, and peoples, and tongues, standing before the throne, and in sight of the Lamb, clothed with white robes, and palms in their hands:

14b He said to me: These are they who are come out of great tribulation, and have washed their robes, and have made them white in the blood of the Lamb.

15 Therefore they are before the throne of God, and they serve him day and night in his temple: and he, that sitteth on the throne, shall dwell over them.

16 They shall no more hunger nor thirst, neither shall the sun fall on them, nor any heat.

17 For the Lamb, which is in the midst of the throne, shall rule them, and shall lead them to the fountains of the waters of life, and God shall wipe away all tears from their eyes.

The second reading from Revelation presents a vision of a vast multitude from every nation, tribe, and people group. These people are clothed in white robes and stand before the throne of God. They have come out of great tribulation, and God himself tends to their needs. This passage offers a glimpse of heaven and the eternal reward that awaits those who are faithful to God.

Alleluia: John 10: 14

R. Alleluia, alleluia.

14 I am the good shepherd, says the Lord; I know my sheep, and mine know me.

R. Alleluia, alleluia.

The Good Shepherd (John 10: 27-30):

27 My sheep hear my voice: and I know them, and they follow me.

28 And I give them life everlasting; and they shall not perish for ever, and no man shall pluck them out of my hand.

29 That which my Father hath given me, is greater than all: and no one can snatch them out of the hand of my Father.

30 **I and the Father are one.**

The Gospel of John presents the metaphor of Jesus as the Good Shepherd. He knows his sheep and they know him. He is willing to lay down his life for them, unlike hired hands who would flee in the face of danger. This passage emphasizes the close relationship between Jesus and his followers, built on trust, love, and protection.

Reflect & Respond:

- How does the story of Paul and Barnabas in Acts inspire you to share your faith with others, even those outside your immediate circle?

- Consider the image of the multitude in Revelation. Does this passage bring you comfort or hope? Why?

- The metaphor of the Good Shepherd is a cornerstone of Christian belief. How does this image impact your understanding of your relationship with Jesus?

Prayer:

Dear God, thank you for your love and faithfulness. We are grateful for the gift of being your sheep, under the care of your watchful eye. Help us to hear your voice and follow your guidance. May we know the depths of your love and share it with the world. Amen.

Challenge:

This week, reach out to a fellow Christian and share a conversation about your faith. Discuss what the image of the Good Shepherd means to you both. You can also reflect on how you can better live out your role as part of Jesus' flock, supporting and encouraging one another.

Notes:_____
_____
_____

Sunday, May 18

- Fifth Sunday of Easter

First Reading: Acts 14: 21-27

Responsorial Psalm: Psalms 145: 8-9, 10-11, 12-13

Second Reading: Revelation 21: 1-5a

Alleluia: John 13: 34

Gospel: John 13: 31-33a, 34-35

Lectionary: 54

This Fifth Sunday of Easter, also sometimes known as Cantate Sunday, emphasizes the importance of love as the central message of Christianity. The readings call us to love one another as Jesus has loved us, a love that is sacrificial, selfless, and enduring.

Paul and Barnabas Return to Antioch (Acts 14: 21-27):

21 And when they had preached the gospel to that city, and had taught many, they returned again to Lystra, and to Iconium, and to Antioch:

22 Confirming the souls of the disciples, and exhorting them to continue in the faith: and that through many tribulations we must enter into the kingdom of God.

23 And when they had ordained to them priests in every church, and had prayed with fasting, they commended them to the Lord, in whom they believed.

24 And passing through Pisidia, they came into Pamphylia.

25 And having spoken the word of the Lord in Perge, they went down into Attalia:

26 And thence they sailed to Antioch, from whence they had been delivered to the grace of God, unto the work which they accomplished.

27 And when they were come, and had assembled the church, they related what great things God had done with them, and how he had opened the door of faith to the Gentiles.

The first reading from Acts recounts Paul and Barnabas returning to Antioch after their missionary journey. They share stories of their experiences and the encouraging response they received from Gentiles. This passage highlights the growth of the early church and the importance of sharing the gospel message.

Responsorial Psalm: Psalms 145: 8-9, 10-11, 12-13

R. (1) I will praise your name for ever, my king and my God.
or
R. Alleluia.
8 The Lord is gracious and merciful: patient and plenteous in mercy.
9 The Lord is sweet to all: and his tender mercies are over all his works.
R. I will praise your name for ever, my king and my God.
or
R. Alleluia.

10 Let all thy works, O lord, praise thee: and let thy saints bless thee.
11 They shall speak of the glory of thy kingdom: and shall tell of thy power:
R. I will praise your name for ever, my king and my God.
or
R. Alleluia.
12 To make thy might known to the sons of men: and the glory of the magnificence of thy kingdom.

13 Thy kingdom is a kingdom of all ages: and thy dominion endureth throughout all generations. The Lord is faithful in all his words: and holy in all his works.

R. I will praise your name for ever, my king and my God.

or

R. Alleluia.

A New Heaven and New Earth (Revelation 21: 1-5a):

1 And I saw a new heaven and a new earth. For the first heaven and the first earth was gone, and the sea is now no more.

2 And I John saw the holy city, the new Jerusalem, coming down out of heaven from God, prepared as a bride adorned for her husband.

3 And I heard a great voice from the throne, saying: Behold the tabernacle of God with men, and he will dwell with them. And they shall be his people; and God himself with them shall be their God.

4 And God shall wipe away all tears from their eyes: and death shall be no more, nor mourning, nor crying, nor sorrow shall be any more, for the former things are passed away.

5a And he that sat on the throne, said: Behold, I make all things new.

The second reading from Revelation offers a glimpse of a new heaven and a new earth, where God will dwell with his people. There will be no more pain or suffering, and God will wipe away all tears from their eyes. This passage provides a vision of hope and the ultimate fulfillment of God's promises.

Alleluia: John 13: 34

R. Alleluia, alleluia.

34 I give you a new commandment, says the Lord: love one another as I have loved you.

R. Alleluia, alleluia.

The New Commandment (John 13: 31-33a, 34-35):

31 When he therefore was gone out, Jesus said: Now is the Son of man glorified, and God is glorified in him.

32 If God be glorified in him, God also will glorify him in himself; and immediately will he glorify him.

33 Little children, yet a little while I am with you. You shall seek me; and as I said to the Jews: Whither I go you cannot come; so I say to you now.

34 A new commandment I give unto you: That you love one another, as I have loved you, that you also love one another.

35 By this shall all men know that you are my disciples, if you have love one for another.

The Gospel of John presents Jesus' new commandment: "Love one another as I have loved you." This love is not based on emotions or feelings, but on a commitment to act in the best interests of others, just as Jesus laid down his life for us. This commandment becomes the identifying mark of Jesus' disciples.

loved us, with compassion, forgiveness, and selflessness. May our love be a reflection of your love in the world, a beacon of hope and a testament to your teachings. Amen.

Reflect & Respond:

- How does the story of Paul and Barnabas in Acts inspire you to share your faith with others?

- Consider the image of the new heaven and new earth in Revelation. What does this passage mean to you?

- Jesus' commandment to love one another is central to the Christian faith. How can you better embody this love in your daily interactions with others?

Prayer:

Dear God, fill our hearts with your love. Grant us the strength to love one another as you have

Challenge:

This week, perform a random act of kindness for someone you don't know well, or even for someone you may not particularly like. This could be anything from offering a helping hand to simply offering a smile or a kind word. Remember, love can bridge differences and create positive connections in unexpected ways.

Notes:_____

_____

_____

_____

_____

_____

_____

_____

Sunday, May 25

- Sixth Sunday of Easter

First Reading: Acts 15: 1-2, 22-29

Responsorial Psalm: Psalms 67: 2-3, 5, 6 and 8

Second Reading: Revelation 21: 10-14, 22-23

Alleluia: John 14: 23

Gospel: John 14: 23-29

Lectionary: 57

This Sixth Sunday of Easter focuses on the themes of peace and the coming of the Holy Spirit. The readings offer comfort, hope, and a reminder of the ongoing presence of God in our lives.

The Jerusalem Council (Acts 15: 1-2, 22-29):

1 And some coming down from Judea, taught the brethren: That except you be circumcised after the manner of Moses, you cannot be saved.

2 And when Paul and Barnabas had no small contest with them, they determined that Paul and Barnabas, and certain others of the other side, should go up to the apostles and priests to Jerusalem about this question.

22 Then it pleased the apostles and ancients, with the whole church, to choose men of their own company, and to send to Antioch, with Paul and Barnabas, namely, Judas, who was surnamed Barsabas, and Silas, chief men among the brethren.

23 Writing by their hands: The apostles and ancients, brethren, to the brethren of the Gentiles that are at Antioch, and in Syria and Cilicia, greeting.

24 Forasmuch as we have heard, that some going out from us have troubled you with words, subverting your souls; to whom we gave no commandment:

25 It hath seemed good to us, being assembled together, to choose out

men, and to send them unto you, with our well beloved Barnabas and Paul:

26 Men that have given their lives for the name of our Lord Jesus Christ.

27 We have sent therefore Judas and Silas, who themselves also will, by word of mouth, tell you the same things.

28 For it hath seemed good to the Holy Ghost and to us, to lay no further burden upon you than these necessary things:

29 That you abstain from things sacrificed to idols, and from blood, and from things strangled, and from fornication; from which things keeping yourselves, you shall do well. Fare ye well.

The first reading from Acts recounts the Jerusalem Council, a gathering of early church leaders to discuss the issue of Gentile converts. The council ultimately decides that Gentiles do not need to follow all the Jewish laws in order to be Christians. This passage highlights the evolving nature of the early church and its openness to new people and ideas.

Responsorial Psalm: Psalms 67: 2-3, 5, 6 and 8

R. (4) O God, let all the nations praise you!
or
R. Alleluia.
2 May God have mercy on us, and bless us: may he cause the light of his countenance to shine upon us, and may he have mercy on us.
3 That we may know thy way upon earth: thy salvation in all nations.
R. O God, let all the nations praise you!
or
R. Alleluia.
5 Let the nations be glad and rejoice: for thou judgest the people with justice, and directest the nations upon earth.
R. O God, let all the nations praise you!
or
R. Alleluia.

6 Let the people, O God, confess to thee: let all the people give praise to thee:

8 May God bless us: and all the ends of the earth fear him.

R. O God, let all the nations praise you!

or

R. Alleluia.

The New Jerusalem (Revelation 21: 10-14, 22-23):

10 And he took me up in spirit to a great and high mountain: and he shewed me the holy city Jerusalem coming down out of heaven from God,

11 Having the glory of God, and the light thereof was like to a precious stone, as to the jasper stone, even as crystal.

12 And it had a wall great and high, having twelve gates, and in the gates twelve angels, and names written thereon, which are the names of the twelve tribes of the children of Israel.

13 On the east, three gates: and on the north, three gates: and on the south, three gates: and on the west, three gates.

14 And the wall of the city had twelve foundations, and in them, the twelve names of the twelve apostles of the Lamb.

22 And I saw no temple therein. For the Lord God Almighty is the temple thereof, and the Lamb.

23 And the city hath no need of the sun, nor of the moon, to shine in it. For the glory of God hath enlightened it, and the Lamb is the lamp thereof.

The second reading from Revelation presents a beautiful description of the New Jerusalem, a dazzling city of gold and jewels. This city symbolizes the ultimate fulfillment of God's plan for his people, a place of peace, beauty, and perfection.

Alleluia: John 14: 23

R. Alleluia, alleluia.

23 Whoever loves me will keep my word, says the Lord, and my Father will love him and we will come to him.

R. Alleluia, alleluia.

Peace I Leave With You (John 14: 23-29):

23 Jesus answered, and said to him: If any one love me, he will keep my word, and my Father will love him, and we will come to him, and will make our abode with him.

24 He that loveth me not, keepeth not my words. And the word which you have heard, is not mine; but the Father's who sent me.

25 These things have I spoken to you, abiding with you.

26 But the Paraclete, the Holy Ghost, whom the Father will send in my name, he will teach you all things, and bring all things to your mind, whatsoever I shall have said to you.

27 Peace I leave with you, my peace I give unto you: not as the world giveth, do I give unto you. Let not your heart be troubled, nor let it be afraid.

28 You have heard that I said to you: I go away, and I come unto you. If you loved me, you would indeed be glad, because I go to the Father: for the Father is greater than I.

29 And now I have told you before it comes to pass: that when it shall come to pass, you may believe.

The Gospel of John features Jesus' comforting words to his disciples during the Last Supper. He assures them that he is leaving them with peace, not the kind of peace the world gives, but a deep and abiding peace that comes from knowing God. Jesus also promises to send the Holy Spirit, the Advocate, who will teach them all things and remind them of everything he has said.

Reflect & Respond:

- How does the story of the Jerusalem Council in Acts demonstrate the adaptability of the early church?

- Consider the image of the New Jerusalem in Revelation. What aspects of this description bring you hope or comfort?

- Jesus' message of peace is especially relevant in times of difficulty. How can you cultivate a sense of peace in your own life, even amidst challenges?

Prayer:

Dear God, grant us your peace, which surpasses all understanding. Fill our hearts with hope for the future and the promise of the New Jerusalem. May the Holy Spirit be our guide and comforter, reminding us of your love and presence in all that we do. Amen.

Challenge:

This week, take some time for quiet reflection or meditation. Focus on letting go of worries and anxieties, and instead cultivate a sense of inner peace. You can also reach out to someone who may be struggling and offer them words of encouragement or simply a listening ear. By sharing peace with others, we can create a ripple effect of hope and comfort in the world.

Notes:_____

June 2025

Sunday, June 1

- **Seventh Sunday of Easter**

- **Ascension of the Lord - Solemnity**

First Reading: Acts 1: 1-11

Responsorial Psalm: Psalms 47: 2-3, 6-7, 8-9

Second Reading: Ephesians 1: 17-23 or Hebrews 9: 24-28; 10: 19-23

Alleluia: Matthew 28: 19a, 20b

Gospel: Luke 24: 46-53

Lectionary: 58

Please note: The Ascension of the Lord is typically celebrated on the Thursday following the Sixth Sunday of Easter. However, in some US dioceses (including Alaska, California, Hawaii, Idaho, Montana, Nevada, Oregon, Utah, and Washington), it is observed on the following Sunday, June 1st in this case.

This feast day commemorates Jesus' ascension into heaven, marking the end of his earthly ministry and the beginning of his reign at the right hand of the Father. The readings highlight the promise of Jesus' return and the ongoing presence of the Holy Spirit.

The Promise of the Holy Spirit (Acts 1: 1-11):

1 The former treatise I made, O Theophilus, of all things which Jesus began to do and to teach,

2 Until the day on which, giving commandments by the Holy Ghost to the apostles whom he had chosen, he was taken up.

3 To whom also he shewed himself alive after his passion, by many proofs, for forty days appearing to them, and speaking of the kingdom of God.

4 And eating together with them, he commanded them, that they should not depart from Jerusalem, but should wait for the promise of the Father, which you have heard (saith he) by my mouth.

5 For John indeed baptized with water, but you shall be baptized with the Holy Ghost, not many days hence.

6 They therefore who were come together, asked him, saying: Lord, wilt thou at this time restore again the kingdom to Israel?

7 But he said to them: It is not for you to know the times or moments, which the Father hath put in his own power:

8 But you shall receive the power of the Holy Ghost coming upon you, and you shall be witnesses unto me in Jerusalem, and in all Judea, and Samaria, and even to the uttermost part of the earth.

9 And when he had said these things, while they looked on, he was raised up: and a cloud received him out of their sight.

10 And while they were beholding him going up to heaven, behold two men stood by them in white garments.

11 Who also said: Ye men of Galilee, why stand you looking up to heaven? This Jesus who is taken up from you into heaven, shall so come, as you have seen him going into heaven.

The first reading from Acts recounts Jesus' final instructions to his disciples before he ascends into heaven. He promises to send the Holy Spirit, who will empower them to be his witnesses in Jerusalem and to the ends of the earth. This passage marks the beginning of the Church's mission to spread the gospel message to the world.

Responsorial Psalm: Psalms 47: 2-3, 6-7, 8-9

R. (6) God mounts his throne to shouts of joy: a blare of trumpets for the Lord.
or
R. Alleluia.
2 O clap your hands, all ye nations: shout unto God with the voice of Joy,

3 For the Lord is high, terrible: a great king over all the earth.

R. God mounts his throne to shouts of joy: a blare of trumpets for the Lord.

or

R. Alleluia.

6 God is ascended with jubilee, and the Lord with the sound of trumpet.

7 Sing praises to our God, sing ye: sing praises to our king, sing ye.

R. God mounts his throne to shouts of joy: a blare of trumpets for the Lord.

or

R. Alleluia.

8 For God is the king of all the earth: sing ye wisely.

9 God shall reign over the nations: God sitteth on his holy throne.

R. God mounts his throne to shouts of joy: a blare of trumpets for the Lord.

or

R. Alleluia.

Unity in Christ (Ephesians 1: 17-23) or The High Priest and the New Covenant (Hebrews 9: 24-28; 10: 19-23):

17 That the God of our Lord Jesus Christ, the Father of glory, may give unto you the spirit of wisdom and of revelation, in the knowledge of him:

18 The eyes of your heart enlightened, that you may know what the hope is of the glory of his inheritance in the saints.

19 And what is the exceeding greatness of his power towards us, who believe according to the operation of the might of his power,

20 Which he wrought in Christ, raising him up from the dead, and setting him on his right hand in the heavenly places.

21 Above all principality, and power, and virtue, and dominion, and every name that is named, not only in this world, but also in that which is to come.

22 And he hath subjected all things under his feet, and hath made him head over all the church,

23 Which is his body, and the fulness of him who is filled all in all.

Or

24 For Jesus is not entered into the holies made with hands, the patterns of the true: but into heaven itself, that he may appear now in the presence of God for us.

25 Nor yet that he should offer himself often, as the high priest entereth into the holies, every year with the blood of others:

26 For then he ought to have suffered often from the beginning of the world: but now once at the end of ages, he hath appeared for the destruction of sin, by the sacrifice of himself.

27 And as it is appointed unto men once to die, and after this the judgment:

28 So also Christ was offered once to exhaust the sins of many; the second time he shall appear without sin to them that expect him unto salvation.

10:19 Having therefore, brethren, a confidence in the entering into the holies by the blood of Christ;

20 A new and living way which he hath dedicated for us through the veil, that is to say, his flesh,

21 And a high priest over the house of God:

22 Let us draw near with a true heart in fulness of faith, having our hearts sprinkled from an evil conscience, and our bodies washed with clean water.

23 Let us hold fast the confession of our hope without wavering (for he is faithful that hath promised),

The second reading offers a choice between two passages. Ephesians emphasizes the unity that believers have in Christ, who is the head of the church. Hebrews focuses on Jesus' role as the high priest who has entered the heavenly sanctuary, making a sacrifice for our sins. Both passages connect the Ascension to Jesus' ongoing work of intercession and his role as our mediator with God.

Alleluia: Matthew 28: 19a, 20b

R. Alleluia, alleluia.

19a, 20b Go and teach all nations, says the Lord; I am with you always, until the end of the world.

R. Alleluia, alleluia.

Jesus Ascends into Heaven (Luke 24: 46-53):

46 And he said to them: Thus it is written, and thus it behoved Christ to suffer, and to rise again from the dead, the third day:

47 And that penance and remission of sins should be preached in his name, unto all nations, beginning at Jerusalem.

48 And you are witnesses of these things.

49 And I send the promise of my Father upon you: but stay you in the city till you be endued with power from on high.

50 And he led them out as far as Bethania: and lifting up his hands, he blessed them.

51 And it came to pass, whilst he blessed them, he departed from them, and was carried up to heaven.

52 And they adoring went back into Jerusalem with great joy.

53 And they were always in the temple, praising and blessing God. Amen.

The Gospel of Luke presents the account of Jesus' ascension. He leads his disciples out to Bethany, and as he blesses them, he is lifted up into heaven. A cloud takes him out of their sight, and two angels appear, assuring the disciples that Jesus will return in the same way he has left. This passage marks the culmination of Jesus' earthly ministry and offers a promise of his return.

Reflect & Respond:

- How does the story of Jesus' final instructions to his disciples in Acts fill you with hope for the future of the Church?

- Consider the concept of Jesus' role as high priest or the unity we have in Christ. How does this concept impact your understanding of your relationship with God and other believers?

- The Ascension of the Lord marks the end of Jesus' physical presence on Earth. How can you continue to experience Jesus' presence in your daily life?

Prayer:

Dear God, we celebrate the glorious ascension of your Son, Jesus Christ, into heaven. Thank you for the promise of the Holy Spirit and the hope of your Son's return. May we continue to be your witnesses in the world, sharing your love and message with all we encounter. Amen.

Challenge:

This week, reflect on your own role as a witness for Christ. How can you share your faith with others, both in words and actions? Look for opportunities to live out your faith in your daily interactions, demonstrating God's love

through your kindness and compassion.

Notes:_____
_____
_____
_____
_____
_____
_____
_____
_____
_____
_____
_____
_____
_____
_____
_____
_____
_____
_____
_____
_____
_____
_____
_____
_____
_____

Sunday, June 8

- **Pentecost - Solemnity**

First Reading: Acts 2: 1-11

Responsorial Psalm: Psalms 104: 1, 24, 29-30, 31, 34

Second Reading: First Corinthians 12: 3b-7, 12-13 or Romans 8: 8-17

Gospel: John 20: 19-23 or John 14: 15-16, 23b-26

Lectionary: 63

Pentecost, also known as Whitsunday, is a joyous celebration that marks the descent of the Holy Spirit upon the Apostles and the birth of the Christian Church. The readings emphasize the power of the Holy Spirit to empower believers, guide them in truth, and unite them in faith.

The Holy Spirit Descends (Acts 2: 1-11):

1 And when the days of the Pentecost were accomplished, they were all together in one place:

2 And suddenly there came a sound from heaven, as of a mighty wind coming, and it filled the whole house where they were sitting.

3 And there appeared to them parted tongues as it were of fire, and it sat upon every one of them:

4 And they were all filled with the Holy Ghost, and they began to speak with divers tongues, according as the Holy Ghost gave them to speak.

5 Now there were dwelling at Jerusalem, Jews, devout men, out of every nation under heaven.

6 And when this was noised abroad, the multitude came together, and were confounded in mind, because that every man heard them speak in his own tongue.

7 And they were all amazed, and wondered, saying: Behold, are not all these, that speak, Galileans?

8 And how have we heard, every man our own tongue wherein we were born?

9 Parthians, and Medes, and Elamites, and inhabitants of Mesopotamia, Judea, and Cappadocia, Pontus and Asia,

10 Phrygia, and Pamphylia, Egypt, and the parts of Libya about Cyrene, and strangers of Rome,

11 Jews also, and proselytes, Cretes, and Arabians: we have heard them speak in our own tongues the wonderful works of God.

The first reading from Acts recounts the dramatic event of Pentecost. As the disciples are gathered together, a sound like a rushing wind fills the room, and tongues of fire appear above their heads. They are filled with the Holy Spirit and begin to speak in different languages, enabling them to share the gospel message with people from all nations. This passage marks the beginning of the Church's mission to spread the gospel to the world.

Responsorial Psalm: Psalms 104: 1, 24, 29-30, 31, 34

R. (30) Lord, send out your Spirit, and renew the face of the earth.
or
R. Alleluia.
1 Bless the Lord, O my soul: O Lord my God, thou art exceedingly great. Thou hast put on praise and beauty:
24 How great are thy works, O Lord? thou hast made all things in wisdom: the earth is filled with thy riches.
R. **Lord, send out your Spirit, and renew the face of the earth.**
or
R. Alleluia.
29 But if thou turnest away thy face, they shall be troubled: thou shalt take away their breath, and they shall fail, and shall return to their dust.
30 Thou shalt send forth thy spirit, and they shall be created: and thou shalt renew the face of the earth.

R. Lord, send out your Spirit, and renew the face of the earth.

or

R. Alleluia.

31 May the glory of the Lord endure for ever: the Lord shall rejoice in his works.

34 Let my speech be acceptable to him: but I will take delight in the Lord.

R. Lord, send out your Spirit, and renew the face of the earth.

or

R. Alleluia.

Gifts of the Holy Spirit (1 Corinthians 12: 3b-7, 12-13) or The Spirit Gives Life (Romans 8: 8-17):

3b No man can say the Lord Jesus, but by the Holy Ghost.

4 Now there are diversities of graces, but the same Spirit;

5 And there are diversities of ministries, but the same Lord;

6 And there are diversities of operations, but the same God, who worketh all in all.

7 And the manifestation of the Spirit is given to every man unto profit.

12 For as the body is one, and hath many members; and all the members of the body, whereas they are many, yet are one body, so also is Christ.

13 For in one Spirit were we all baptized into one body, whether Jews or Gentiles, whether bond or free; and in one Spirit we have all been made to drink.

Or

8 And they who are in the flesh, cannot please God.

9 But you are not in the flesh, but in the spirit, if so be that the Spirit of God dwell in you. Now if any man have not the Spirit of Christ, he is none of his.

10 And if Christ be in you, the body indeed is dead, because of sin; but the spirit liveth, because of justification.

11 And if the Spirit of him that raised up Jesus from the dead, dwell in you; he that raised up Jesus Christ from the dead, shall quicken also your mortal bodies, because of his Spirit that dwelleth in you.

12 Therefore, brethren, we are debtors, not to the flesh, to live according to the flesh.

13 For if you live according to the flesh, you shall die: but if by the Spirit you mortify the deeds of the flesh, you shall live.

14 For whosoever are led by the Spirit of God, they are the sons of God.

15 For you have not received the spirit of bondage again in fear; but you have received the spirit of adoption of sons, whereby we cry: Abba (Father).

16 For the Spirit himself giveth testimony to our spirit, that we are the sons of God.

17 And if sons, heirs also; heirs indeed of God, and joint heirs with Christ: yet so, if we suffer with him, that we may be also glorified with him.

The second reading offers a choice between two passages. 1 Corinthians emphasizes the diversity of gifts that the Holy Spirit bestows on believers, all for the common good. Romans focuses on the role of the Holy Spirit in giving life to our mortal bodies and guiding us as children of God. Both passages highlight the empowering and transformative work of the Holy Spirit in the lives of believers.

Alleluia

R. Alleluia, alleluia.

Come, Holy Spirit, fill the hearts of your faithful and kindle in them the fire of your love.

R. Alleluia, alleluia.

The Coming of the Holy Spirit (John 20: 19-23) or The Advocate (John 14: 15-16, 23b-26):

19 Now when it was late that same day, the first of the week, and the doors were shut, where the disciples were gathered together, for fear of the Jews, Jesus came and stood in the midst, and said to them: Peace be to you.

20 And when he had said this, he shewed them his hands and his side. The disciples therefore were glad, when they saw the Lord.

21 He said therefore to them again: Peace be to you. As the Father hath sent me, I also send you.

22 When he had said this, he breathed on them; and he said to them: Receive ye the Holy Ghost.

23 Whose sins you shall forgive, they are forgiven them; and whose sins you shall retain, they are retained.

Or

15 If you love me, keep my commandments.

16 And I will ask the Father, and he shall give you another Paraclete, that he may abide with you for ever.

23b If any one love me, he will keep my word, and my Father will love him, and we will come to him, and will make our abode with him.

24 He that loveth me not, keepeth not my words. And the word which you have heard, is not mine; but the Father's who sent me.

25 These things have I spoken to you, abiding with you.

26 But the Paraclete, the Holy Ghost, whom the Father will send in my name, he will teach you all things, and bring all things to your mind, whatsoever I shall have said to you.

The Gospel of John offers a choice between two passages. John 20 recounts Jesus appearing to his disciples after the resurrection and breathing on them, saying, "Receive the Holy Spirit." John 14 presents Jesus' promise to send the Advocate, the Holy Spirit, who will teach them all things and remind them of everything he has said. Both passages connect the coming of the Holy Spirit to Jesus' ongoing presence and guidance in the lives of his disciples.

Reflect & Respond:

- How does the story of Pentecost in Acts fill you with hope and excitement about the power of the Holy Spirit?

- Consider the concept of the gifts of the Holy Spirit. Do you have any particular gifts that you believe the Holy Spirit has bestowed upon you? How can you use those gifts to serve God and others?

- The Holy Spirit is a comforter, a guide, and a source of power. How can you be more open to the leading of the Holy Spirit in your own life?

Prayer:

Dear God, on this Pentecost Sunday, we celebrate the descent of the Holy Spirit upon your disciples. Fill us afresh with your Spirit, empowering us to be your witnesses in the world. Grant us the gifts of the Spirit so that we can build up your Church and share your love with all we encounter. Amen.

Challenge:

This week, spend some time in prayer, asking the Holy Spirit to fill you with his gifts. Discern how you can use those gifts to serve others and build up the body of Christ, the Church. Consider volunteering your time or talents to a ministry or cause that aligns with your passions.

Notes:_____
_____
_____
_____
_____
_____
_____
_____
_____
_____
_____
_____
_____
_____
_____
_____
_____
_____
_____
_____
_____
_____
_____
_____

Sunday, June 15

- The Holy Trinity - Solemnity

First Reading: Proverbs 8: 22-31

Responsorial Psalm: Psalms 8: 4-5, 6-7, 8-9

Second Reading: Romans 5: 1-5

Alleluia: Revelation 1: 8

Gospel: John 16: 12-15

Lectionary: 166

Today is the Solemnity of the Most Holy Trinity, a day dedicated to celebrating the central mystery of the Christian faith: God as one God in three divine persons – Father, Son (Jesus Christ), and Holy Spirit. The readings explore the nature of God and the relationships within the Trinity.

Wisdom's Eternal Role (Proverbs 8: 22-31):

22 The Lord possessed me in the beginning of his ways, before he made any thing from the beginning.

23 I was set up from eternity, and of old before the earth was made.

24 The depths were not as yet, and I was already conceived. neither had the fountains of waters as yet sprung out:

25 The mountains with their huge bulk had not as yet been established: before the hills I was brought forth:

26 He had not yet made the earth, nor the rivers, nor the poles of the world.

27 When he prepared the heavens, I was present: when with a certain law and compass he enclosed the depths:

28 When he established the sky above, and poised the fountains of waters:

29 When he compassed the sea with its bounds, and set a law to the waters that they should not pass

their limits: when be balanced the foundations of the earth;

30 I was with him forming all things: and was delighted every day, playing before him at all times;

31 Playing in the world: and my delights were to be with the children of men.

The first reading from Proverbs presents a poetic personification of wisdom, existing before creation alongside God. This passage can be interpreted as foreshadowing the role of the Word, who became flesh in Jesus Christ.

Responsorial Psalm: Psalms 8: 4-5, 6-7, 8-9

R. (2a) O Lord, our God, how wonderful your name in all the earth!

4 For I will behold thy heavens, the works of thy fingers: the moon and the stars which thou hast founded.

5 What is man that thou art mindful of him? or the son of man that thou visitest him?

R. O Lord, our God, how wonderful your name in all the earth!

6 Thou hast made him a little less than the angels, thou hast crowned him with glory and honour:

7 And hast set him over the works of thy hands.

R. O Lord, our God, how wonderful your name in all the earth!

8 Thou hast subjected all things under his feet, all sheep and oxen: moreover the beasts also of the fields.

9 The birds of the air, and the fishes of the sea, that pass through the paths of the sea.

R. O Lord, our God, how wonderful your name in all the earth!

Peace Through Faith (Romans 5: 1-5):

1 Being justified therefore by faith, let us have peace with God, through our Lord Jesus Christ:

2 By whom also we have access through faith into this grace, wherein we stand, and glory in the hope of the glory of the sons of God.

3 And not only so; but we glory also in tribulations, knowing that tribulation worketh patience;

4 And patience trial; and trial hope;

5 And hope confoundeth not: because the charity of God is poured forth in our hearts, by the Holy Ghost, who is given to us.

The second reading from Romans emphasizes the peace and hope we have through faith in Jesus Christ. This peace is a gift from God, made possible by the sacrifice of his Son.

Alleluia: Revelation 1: 8

R. Alleluia, alleluia.

8 Glory to the Father, the Son, and the Holy Spirit; to God who is, who was, and who is to come.

R. Alleluia, alleluia.

The Work of the Holy Spirit (John 16: 12-15):

12 I have yet many things to say to you: but you cannot bear them now.

13 But when he, the Spirit of truth, is come, he will teach you all truth. For he shall not speak of himself;

but what things soever he shall hear, he shall speak; and the things that are to come, he shall shew you.

14 He shall glorify me; because he shall receive of mine, and shall shew it to you.

15 All things whatsoever the Father hath, are mine. Therefore I said, that he shall receive of mine, and shew it to you.

The Gospel of John presents Jesus' words to his disciples during the Last Supper. He speaks of the Holy Spirit, who will come and "guide you into all truth." The Holy Spirit will glorify Jesus and reveal things to come. This passage highlights the role of the Holy Spirit as the comforter, teacher, and ongoing revealer of God's truth.

Reflect & Respond:

- How does the reading from Proverbs challenge you to think about the nature of God?

- Consider the concept of peace through faith in

Romans. How does this concept impact your approach to life's challenges?

- The Holy Spirit is a vital part of the Trinity. How can you cultivate a closer relationship with the Holy Spirit in your daily life?

Prayer:

Dear God, we praise you, Father, Son, and Holy Spirit, one God in three persons. Thank you for revealing your love and mystery to us. Grant us the wisdom to understand you more deeply and the grace to live in communion with you. Amen.

Challenge:

This week, spend some time reflecting on the Trinity. There are many resources available online or at your local library that can help you explore this theological concept further. You can also engage in creative endeavors, such as writing, art, or music, to express your own understanding of the Trinity.

Notes:_____
_____
_____
_____
_____
_____
_____
_____
_____
_____
_____
_____
_____
_____
_____
_____
_____
_____
_____
_____
_____
_____
_____
_____
_____

Sunday, June 22

- Twelfth Sunday in Ordinary Time
- In the United States The Body and Blood of Christ (Corpus Christi) - Solemnity

First Reading: Genesis 14: 18-20

Responsorial Psalm: Psalms 110: 1, 2, 3, 4

Second Reading: First Corinthians 11: 23-26

Alleluia: John 6: 51

Gospel: Luke 9: 11b-17

Lectionary: 169

Please note: While this Sunday is the Twelfth Sunday in Ordinary Time in most parts of the world, in the United States, it is observed as the Solemnity of the Most Holy Body and Blood of Christ, also known as Corpus Christi.

This feast celebrates the Eucharist, the sacrament of bread and wine that is believed to be truly the body and blood of Jesus Christ. The readings focus on themes of sacrifice, covenant, and the Eucharist as a source of spiritual nourishment.

Melchizedek, King of Salem (Genesis 14: 18-20):

18 But Melchisedech the king of Salem, bringing forth bread and wine, for he was the priest of the most high God,

19 Blessed him, and said: Blessed be Abram by the most high God, who created heaven and earth.

20 And blessed be the most high God, by whose protection the enemies are in thy hands. And he gave him the tithes of all.

The first reading from Genesis tells the story of Melchizedek, king of Salem, who brings out bread and wine to bless Abram (later renamed Abraham) after his victory in battle. Melchizedek is seen as a prefiguration of Christ, the eternal priest who offers himself as a sacrifice.

Responsorial Psalm: Psalms 110: 1, 2, 3, 4

R. (4b) You are a priest forever, in the line of Melchizedek.

1 The Lord said to my Lord: Sit thou at my right hand: Until I make thy enemies thy footstool.

R. You are a priest forever, in the line of Melchizedek.

2 The Lord will send forth the sceptre of thy power out of Sion: rule thou in the midst of thy enemies.

R. You are a priest forever, in the line of Melchizedek.

3 With thee is the principality in the day of thy strength: in the brightness of the saints: from the womb before the day star I begot thee.

R. You are a priest forever, in the line of Melchizedek.

4 The Lord hath sworn, and he will not repent: Thou art a priest for ever according to the order of Melchisedech.

R. You are a priest forever, in the line of Melchizedek.

The Institution of the Lord's Supper (1 Corinthians 11: 23-26):

23 For I have received of the Lord that which also I delivered unto you, that the Lord Jesus, the same night in which he was betrayed, took bread.

24 And giving thanks, broke, and said: Take ye, and eat: this is my body, which shall be delivered for you: this do for the commemoration of me.

25 In like manner also the chalice, after he had supped, saying: This chalice is the new testament in my blood: this do ye, as often as you shall drink, for the commemoration of me.

26 For as often as you shall eat this bread, and drink the chalice, you

shall shew the death of the Lord, until he come.

The second reading from 1 Corinthians recounts Paul's description of the Last Supper. Jesus institutes the Eucharist, instructing his disciples to do this in remembrance of him. The bread and the cup become symbols of his body and blood, a sacred meal that nourishes believers and strengthens their covenant with God.

Alleluia: John 6: 51

R. Alleluia, alleluia.

51 I am the living bread that came down from heaven, says the Lord; whoever eats this bread will live forever.

R. Alleluia, alleluia.

The Feeding of the Five Thousand (Luke 9: 11b-17):

11b Jesus spoke to them of the kingdom of God, and healed them who had need of healing.

12 Now the day began to decline. And the twelve came and said to him: Send away the multitude, that going into the towns and villages round about, they may lodge and get victuals; for we are here in a desert place.

13 But he said to them: Give you them to eat. And they said: We have no more than five loaves and two fishes; unless perhaps we should go and buy food for all this multitude.

14 Now there were about five thousand men. And he said to his disciples: Make them sit down by fifties in a company.

15 And they did so; and made them all sit down.

16 And taking the five loaves and the two fishes, he looked up to heaven, and blessed them; and he broke, and distributed to his disciples, to set before the multitude.

17 And they did all eat, and were filled. And there were taken up of fragments that remained to them, twelve baskets.

The Gospel of Luke presents the story of Jesus feeding the five thousand with five loaves of bread and two fish. This miracle foreshadows the Eucharist, where Jesus offers himself as the bread of life that satisfies our deepest hunger.

Reflect & Respond:

- How does the story of Melchizedek foreshadow the role of Jesus as the eternal priest?

- Consider the significance of the Last Supper as described in 1 Corinthians. How does your understanding of the Eucharist impact your participation in Mass?

- The feeding of the five thousand is a powerful image of Jesus' provision. How does this story impact your faith and trust in God's ability to meet your needs?

Prayer:

Dear God, we thank you for the gift of the Eucharist, your body and blood given for our salvation. Grant us faith to believe in the mystery of your presence in this sacrament. May we be nourished by your love and strengthened to live as your disciples. Amen.

Challenge:

This week, reflect on your own relationship with the Eucharist. Consider attending Mass more regularly or participating in Eucharistic Adoration, a time of prayer and quiet reflection before the Blessed Sacrament. You can also learn more about the theology of the Eucharist or discuss its significance with a priest or trusted spiritual advisor.

Notes:_____
_____
_____
_____
_____
_____
_____
_____

Sunday, June 29

- Saints Peter and Paul, apostles - Solemnity

First Reading: Acts 12: 1-11

Responsorial Psalm: Psalms 34: 2-3, 4-5, 6-7, 8-9

Second Reading: Second Timothy 4: 6-8, 17-18

Alleluia: Matthew 16: 18

Gospel: Matthew 16: 13-19

Lectionary: 591

Today, we celebrate the solemnity of Saints Peter and Paul, two of the most important figures in Christianity. Peter, the rock on which Jesus promised to build his church, and Paul, the passionate missionary who spread the gospel to the Gentiles, continue to inspire believers today. The readings highlight their courage, faith, and unwavering commitment to Christ.

Peter's Miraculous Rescue (Acts 12: 1-11):

1 And at the same time, Herod the king stretched forth his hands, to afflict some of the church.

2 And he killed James, the brother of John, with the sword.

3 And seeing that it pleased the Jews, he proceeded to take up Peter also. Now it was in the days of the Azymes.

4 And when he had apprehended him, he cast him into prison, delivering him to four files of soldiers to be kept, intending, after the pasch, to bring him forth to the people.

5 Peter therefore was kept in prison. But prayer was made without ceasing by the church unto God for him.

6 And when Herod would have brought him forth, the same night Peter was sleeping between two soldiers, bound with two chains: and the keepers before the door kept the prison.

7 And behold an angel of the Lord stood by him: and a light shined in the room: and he striking Peter on the side, raised him up, saying: Arise quickly. And the chains fell off from his hands.

8 And the angel said to him: Gird thyself, and put on thy sandals. And he did so. And he said to him: Cast thy garment about thee, and follow me.

9 And going out, he followed him, and he knew not that it was true which was done by the angel: but thought he saw a vision.

10 And passing through the first and the second ward, they came to the iron gate that leadeth to the city, which of itself opened to them. And going out, they passed on through one street: and immediately the angel departed from him.

11 And Peter coming to himself, said: Now I know in very deed, that the Lord hath sent his angel, and hath delivered me out of the hand of Herod, and from all the expectation of the people of the Jews.

The first reading from Acts recounts the dramatic story of Peter's miraculous rescue from prison. An angel appears to Peter, frees him from his chains, and leads him out of prison. This passage emphasizes God's power to intervene and protect his followers.

> **Responsorial Psalm: Psalms 34: 2-3, 4-5, 6-7, 8-9**

R. (5) The angel of the Lord will rescue those who fear him.

2 I will bless the Lord at all times, his praise shall be always in my mouth.

3 In the Lord shall my soul be praised: let the meek hear and rejoice.

R. The angel of the Lord will rescue those who fear him.

4 O magnify the Lord with me; and let us extol his name together.

5 I sought the Lord, and he heard me; and he delivered me from all my troubles.

R. The angel of the Lord will rescue those who fear him.

6 Come ye to him and be enlightened: and your faces shall not be confounded.

7 This poor man cried, and the Lord heard him: and saved him out of all his troubles.

R. The angel of the Lord will rescue those who fear him.

8 The angel of the Lord shall encamp round about them that fear him: and shall deliver them.

9 O taste, and see that the Lord is sweet: blessed is the man that hopeth in him.

R. The angel of the Lord will rescue those who fear him.

Paul's Final Words (2 Timothy 4: 6-8, 17-18):

6 For I am even now ready to be sacrificed: and the time of my dissolution is at hand.

7 I have fought a good fight, I have finished my course, I have kept the faith.

8 As to the rest, there is laid up for me a crown of justice, which the Lord the just judge will render to me in that day: and not only to me, but to them also that love his coming. Make haste to come to me quickly.

17 But the Lord stood by me, and strengthened me, that by me the preaching may be accomplished, and that all the Gentiles may hear: and I was delivered out of the mouth of the lion.

18 The Lord hath delivered me from every evil work: and will preserve me unto his heavenly kingdom, to whom be glory for ever and ever. Amen.

The second reading features a portion of Paul's second letter to Timothy. Paul reflects on his life and ministry, expressing confidence that he has fought the good fight and finished the race. He is assured of a crown of righteousness from the Lord. This passage serves as a testament to Paul's unwavering faith and dedication to spreading the gospel.

Alleluia: Matthew 16: 18

R. Alleluia, alleluia.

18 You are Peter and upon this rock I will build my Church, and

the gates of the netherworld shall not prevail against it.

R. Alleluia, alleluia.

The Rock and the Keys (Matthew 16: 13-19):

13 And Jesus came into the quarters of Caesarea Philippi: and he asked his disciples, saying: Whom do men say that the Son of man is?

14 But they said: Some John the Baptist, and other some Elias, and others Jeremias, or one of the prophets.

15 Jesus saith to them: But whom do you say that I am?

16 Simon Peter answered and said: Thou art Christ, the Son of the living God.

17 And Jesus answering, said to him: Blessed art thou, Simon Bar-Jona: because flesh and blood hath not revealed it to thee, but my Father who is in heaven.

18 And I say to thee: That thou art Peter; and upon this rock I will build my church, and the gates of hell shall not prevail against it.

19 And I will give to thee the keys of the kingdom of heaven. And whatsoever thou shalt bind upon earth, it shall be bound also in heaven: and whatsoever thou shalt loose upon earth, it shall be loosed also in heaven.

The Gospel of Matthew presents Jesus' question to his disciples: "Who do you say that I am?" Peter makes the pivotal confession of faith, declaring, "You are the Christ, the Son of the living God." Jesus then praises Peter and declares that he will build his church on this rock, and the gates of Hades will not prevail against it. He entrusts Peter with the "keys of the kingdom of heaven." This passage highlights Peter's role as the leader of the apostles and the foundation of the Church.

Reflect & Respond:

- How does the story of Peter's rescue in Acts demonstrate God's faithfulness to his people?

- Consider Paul's final words in 2 Timothy. What does

this passage teach us about perseverance and living a life of faith?

- Peter's confession of faith is a cornerstone of Christian belief. How can you strengthen your own faith and share it with others?

Prayer:

Dear God, we thank you for the apostles Peter and Paul, whose lives and teachings continue to inspire us. Grant us the courage of Peter to confess our faith and the zeal of Paul to share your gospel message with the world. May we be instruments of your love and peace in all that we do. Amen.

Challenge:

This week, learn more about the lives and ministries of Peter and Paul. Consider reading about them in the Bible or other Christian resources. Reflect on how their example can inspire you to live a more faithful and Christ-centered life. You could also reach out to someone who is struggling in their faith and offer them encouragement or support.

Notes:_____

_____
_____
_____
_____
_____
_____
_____
_____
_____
_____
_____
_____
_____
_____
_____
_____
_____
_____

July 2025

Sunday, July 6

- Fourteenth Sunday in Ordinary Time

First Reading: Isaiah 66: 10-14c

Responsorial Psalm: Psalms 66: 1-3, 4-5, 6-7, 16 and 20

Second Reading: Galatians 6: 14-18

Alleluia: Colossians 3: 15a, 16a

Gospel: Luke 10: 1-12, 17-20

Lectionary: 102

This Sunday's readings focus on themes of discipleship, mission, and the joy that comes from following Jesus. We are called to be instruments of God's love and compassion in the world.

The Lord's Comfort for Zion (Isaiah 66: 10-14c):

10 Rejoice with Jerusalem, and be glad with her, all you that love her: rejoice for joy with her, all you that mourn for her.

11 That you may suck, and be filled with the breasts of her consolations: that you may milk out, and flow with delights, from the abundance of her glory.

12 For thus saith the Lord: Behold I will bring upon her as it were a river of peace, and as an overflowing torrent the glory of the Gentiles, which you shall suck; you shall be carried at the breasts, and upon the knees they shall caress you.

13 As one whom the mother caresseth, so will I comfort you, and you shall be comforted in Jerusalem.

14c You shall see and your heart shall rejoice, and your bones shall flourish like an herb, and the hand of the Lord shall be known to his servants.

The first reading from Isaiah presents a beautiful image of God's comforting presence for his people. He promises to bless them abundantly, just as a mother comforts her child. This passage highlights God's love and faithfulness.

Responsorial Psalm: Psalms 66: 1-3, 4-5, 6-7, 16 and 20

R. (1) Let all the earth cry out to God with joy.

1 Shout with joy to God, all the earth,

2 Sing ye a psalm to his name; give glory to his praise.

3 Say unto God, How terrible are thy works, O Lord!

R. Let all the earth cry out to God with joy.

4 Let all the earth adore thee, and sing to thee: let it sing a psalm to thy name.

5 Come and see the works of God; who is terrible in his counsels over the sons of men.

R. Let all the earth cry out to God with joy.

6 Who turneth the sea into dry land, in the river they shall pass on foot: there shall we rejoice in him.

7 Who by his power ruleth for ever: his eyes behold the nations; let not them that provoke him he exalted in themselves.

R. Let all the earth cry out to God with joy.

16 Come and hear, all ye that fear God, and I will tell you what great things he hath done for my soul.

20 Blessed be God, who hath not turned away my prayer, nor his mercy from me.

R. Let all the earth cry out to God with joy.

Boasting Only in the Cross (Galatians 6: 14-18):

14 But God forbid that I should glory, save in the cross of our Lord Jesus Christ; by whom the world is crucified to me, and I to the world.

15 For in Christ Jesus neither circumcision availeth any thing, nor uncircumcision, but a new creature.

16 And whosoever shall follow this rule, peace on them, and mercy, and upon the Israel of God.

17 From henceforth let no man be troublesome to me; for I bear the marks of the Lord Jesus in my body.

18 The grace of our Lord Jesus Christ be with your spirit, brethren. Amen.

The second reading from Galatians features Paul's words to the church in Galatia. He emphasizes that his only boast is in the cross of Christ, where salvation is found. This passage reminds us that our identity is rooted in Christ and his sacrifice.

Alleluia: Colossians 3: 15a, 16a

R. Alleluia, alleluia.

15a, 16a Let the peace of Christ control your hearts; let the word of Christ dwell in you richly.

R. Alleluia, alleluia.

The Sending Out of the Seventy-Two (Luke 10: 1-12, 17-20):

1 And after these things the Lord appointed also other seventy-two: and he sent them two and two before his face into every city and place whither he himself was to come.

2 And he said to them: The harvest indeed is great, but the labourers are few. Pray ye therefore the Lord of the harvest, that he send labourers into his harvest.

3 Go: Behold I send you as lambs among wolves.

4 Carry neither purse, nor scrip, nor shoes; and salute no man by the way.

5 Into whatsoever house you enter, first say: Peace be to this house.

6 And if the son of peace be there, your peace shall rest upon him; but if not, it shall return to you.

7 And in the same house, remain, eating and drinking such things as they have: for the labourer is worthy of his hire. Remove not from house to house.

8 And into what city soever you enter, and they receive you, eat such things as are set before you.

9 And heal the sick that are therein, and say to them: The kingdom of God is come nigh unto you.

10 But into whatsoever city you enter, and they receive you not, going forth into the streets thereof, say:

11 Even the very dust of your city that cleaveth to us, we wipe off against you. Yet know this, that the kingdom of God is at hand.

12 I say to you, it shall be more tolerable at that day for Sodom, than for that city.

17 And the seventy-two returned with joy, saying: Lord, the devils also are subject to us in thy name.

18 And he said to them: I saw Satan like lightning falling from heaven.

19 Behold, I have given you power to tread upon serpents and scorpions, and upon all the power of the enemy: and nothing shall hurt you.

20 But yet rejoice not in this, that spirits are subject unto you; but rejoice in this, that your names are written in heaven.

The Gospel of Luke presents the story of Jesus sending out seventy-two disciples (or seventy according to some translations) to proclaim the kingdom of God. He instructs them to travel light, trusting in God's provision. The disciples return rejoicing, having experienced the power of God at work in their lives. This passage highlights the importance of spreading the gospel message and the joy that comes from serving God.

Reflect & Respond:

- How does the image of God's comfort in Isaiah impact your understanding of God's character?

- Consider Paul's message in Galatians. What does it mean to boast in the cross of Christ?

- The story of the seventy-two disciples is a call to action. How can you be a more active witness for Christ in your daily life?

Prayer:

Dear God, fill us with your love and compassion. Grant us the courage to share your message of hope with the world. May we be instruments of your peace and healing, following in the

footsteps of your Son, Jesus
Christ. Amen.

Challenge:

This week, consider volunteering
your time or talents to serve
others in your community. This
could be anything from helping
at a local soup kitchen to
mentoring a young person.
Remember, even small acts of
service can make a big
difference. You can also reflect
on your own gifts and abilities,
and how you can use them to
build up the body of Christ, the
Church.

Notes:_____
_____
_____
_____
_____
_____
_____
_____
_____
_____

_____
_____
_____
_____
_____
_____
_____
_____
_____
_____
_____
_____
_____
_____
_____
_____
_____
_____
_____
_____
_____
_____
_____
_____
_____

Sunday, July 13

- Fifteenth Sunday in Ordinary Time

First Reading: Deuteronomy 30: 10-14

Responsorial Psalm: Psalms 69: 14, 17, 30-31, 33-34, 36, 37 or Psalms 19: 8, 9, 10, 11

Second Reading: Colossians 1: 15-20

Alleluia: John 6: 63c, 68c

Gospel: Luke 10: 25-37

Lectionary: 105

This Sunday's readings emphasize the importance of love, compassion, and extending God's love to those in need. The readings call us to see Christ in the faces of those around us, particularly those who are marginalized or overlooked.

The Choice Between Life and Death (Deuteronomy 30: 10-14):

10 Yet so if thou hear the voice of the Lord thy God, and keep his precepts and ceremonies, which are written in this law: and return to the Lord thy God with all thy heart, and with all thy soul.

11 This commandment, that I command thee this day is not above thee, nor far off from thee:

12 Nor is it in heaven, that thou shouldst say: Which of us can go up to heaven to bring it unto us, and we may hear and fulfill it in work?

13 Nor is it beyond the sea: that thou mayst excuse thyself, and say: Which of us can cross the sea, and bring it unto us: that we may hear, and do that which is commanded?

14 But the word is very nigh unto thee, in thy mouth and in thy heart, that thou mayst do it.

The first reading from Deuteronomy presents Moses' words to the Israelites as they prepare to enter the Promised

Land. He reminds them that God's commands are not too difficult or distant, but are close at hand. They have the choice to obey God's commandments and live, or to disobey and die. This passage highlights God's desire for his people to follow his ways and experience his blessings.

Responsorial Psalm: Psalms 69: 14, 17, 30-31, 33-34, 36, 37 or Psalms 19: 8, 9, 10, 11

R. (33) Turn to the Lord in your need, and you will live.
14 But as for me, my prayer is to thee, O Lord; for the time of thy good pleasure, O God. In the multitude of thy mercy hear me, in the truth of thy salvation.
17 Hear me, O Lord, for thy mercy is kind; look upon me according to the multitude of thy tender mercies.
R. Turn to the Lord in your need, and you will live.
30 But I am poor and sorrowful: thy salvation, O God, hath set me up.

31 I will praise the name of God with a canticle: and I will magnify him with praise.
R. Turn to the Lord in your need, and you will live.
33 Let the poor see and rejoice: seek ye God, and your soul shall live.
34 For the Lord hath heard the poor: and hath not despised his prisoners.
R. Turn to the Lord in your need, and you will live.
36 For God will save Sion, and the cities of Juda shall be built up. And they shall dwell there, and acquire it by inheritance.
37 And the seed of his servants shall possess it; and they that love his name shall dwell therein.
R. Turn to the Lord in your need, and you will live.
Or
R. (9a) Your words, Lord, are Spirit and life.
8 The law of the Lord is unspotted, converting souls: the testimony of the Lord is faithful, giving wisdom to little ones.
R. Your words, Lord, are Spirit and life.
9 The justices of the Lord are right, rejoicing hearts: the

commandment of the Lord is lightsome, enlightening the eyes.

R. Your words, Lord, are Spirit and life.

10 The fear of the Lord is holy, enduring for ever and ever: the judgments of the Lord are true, justified in themselves.

R. Your words, Lord, are Spirit and life.

11 More to be desired than gold and many precious stones: and sweeter than honey and the honeycomb.

R. Your words, Lord, are Spirit and life.

The Supremacy of Christ (Colossians 1: 15-20):

15 Who is the image of the invisible God, the firstborn of every creature:

16 For in him were all things created in heaven and on earth, visible and invisible, whether thrones, or dominations, or principalities, or powers: all things were created by him and in him.

17 And he is before all, and by him all things consist.

18 And he is the head of the body, the church, who is the beginning, the firstborn from the dead; that in all things he may hold the primacy:

19 Because in him, it hath well pleased the Father, that all fullness should dwell;

20 And through him to reconcile all things unto himself, making peace through the blood of his cross, both as to the things that are on earth, and the things that are in heaven.

The second reading from Colossians focuses on the supremacy of Christ. He is the firstborn of all creation, and everything in heaven and on earth was created through him and for him. This passage emphasizes Jesus' central role in God's plan for salvation.

Alleluia: John 6: 63c, 68c

R. Alleluia, alleluia.

63c, 68c Your words, Lord, are Spirit and life; you have the words of everlasting life.

R. Alleluia, alleluia.

25 And behold a certain lawyer stood up, tempting him, and saying, Master, what must I do to possess eternal life?

26 But he said to him: What is written in the law? how readest thou?

27 He answering, said: Thou shalt love the Lord thy God with thy whole heart, and with thy whole soul, and with all thy strength, and with all thy mind: and thy neighbour as thyself.

28 And he said to him: Thou hast answered right: this do, and thou shalt live.

29 But he willing to justify himself, said to Jesus: And who is my neighbour?

30 And Jesus answering, said: A certain man went down from Jerusalem to Jericho, and fell among robbers, who also stripped him, and having wounded him went away, leaving him half dead.

31 And it chanced, that a certain priest went down the same way: and seeing him, passed by.

32 In like manner also a Levite, when he was near the place and saw him, passed by.

33 But a certain Samaritan being on his journey, came near him; and seeing him, was moved with compassion.

34 And going up to him, bound up his wounds, pouring in oil and wine: and setting him upon his own beast, brought him to an inn, and took care of him.

35 And the next day he took out two pence, and gave to the host, and said: Take care of him; and whatsoever thou shalt spend over and above, I, at my return, will repay thee.

36 Which of these three, in thy opinion, was neighbour to him that fell among the robbers?

37 But he said: He that shewed mercy to him. And Jesus said to him: Go, and do thou in like manner.

The Gospel of Luke presents the famous Parable of the Good Samaritan. A lawyer asks Jesus what he needs to do to inherit eternal life. Jesus responds with a story about a man who is beaten and robbed by robbers. A priest and a Levite pass by without helping, but a Samaritan, a person from a different ethnicity and religion, stops to care for the injured man. Jesus challenges the lawyer to "go and do likewise." This parable teaches us to love our neighbors, whoever they may be, and to show compassion to those in need.

Reflect & Respond:

- How does the reading from Deuteronomy challenge you to live a life closer to God?

- Consider the message of Colossians about Christ's supremacy. How does this concept impact your understanding of faith?

- The Parable of the Good Samaritan is a powerful call to action. How can you be more loving and compassionate towards others in your daily life?

Prayer:

Dear God, open our hearts to your love and compassion. Help us to see the face of Christ in those around us, especially those who are suffering or in need. May we extend your love and mercy to all, following the example of the Good Samaritan. Amen.

Challenge:

This week, be mindful of opportunities to show compassion to others. This could be something as simple as offering a helping hand to someone who seems overwhelmed or showing kindness to someone who is different from you. Remember, even small acts of love can make a big difference in the lives of others.

Notes:_____
_____
_____
_____

Sunday, July 20

- Sixteenth Sunday in Ordinary Time

First Reading: Genesis 18: 1-10a

Responsorial Psalm: Psalms 15: 2-3ab, 3cd-4, 5

Second Reading: Colossians 1: 24-28

Alleluia: Luke 8: 15

Gospel: Luke 10: 38-42

Lectionary: 108

This week's readings focus on the importance of hospitality, listening to God's voice, and choosing the better part.

Hospitality and Revelation (Genesis 18: 1-10a):

1 And the Lord appeared to him in the vale of Mambre as he was sitting at the door of his tent, in the very heat of the day.

2 And when he had lifted up his eyes, there appeared to him three men standing near him: and as soon as he saw them he ran to meet them from the door of his tent, and adored down to the ground.

3 And he said: Lord, if I have found favour in thy sight, pass not away from thy servant:

4 But I will fetch a little water, and wash ye your feet, and rest ye under the tree.

5 And I will set a morsel of bread, and strengthen ye your heart, afterwards you shall pass on: for therefore are you come aside to your servant. And they said: Do as thou hast spoken.

6 Abraham made haste into the tent to Sara, and said to her: Make haste, temper together three measures of flour, and make cakes upon the hearth.

7 And he himself ran to the herd, and took from thence a calf very tender and very good, and gave it to a young man: who made haste and boiled it.

8 He took also butter and milk, and the calf which he had boiled, and set before them: but he stood by them under the tree.

9 And when they had eaten, they said to him: Where is Sara thy wife? He answered: Lo, she is in the tent.

10a And he said to him: I will return and come to thee at this time, life accompanying and Sara thy wife shall have a son.

The first reading from Genesis tells the story of Abraham's encounter with three visitors. He welcomes them into his tent and offers them food and shelter. These visitors are ultimately revealed to be angels, and Abraham has unknowingly entertained messengers from God. This passage highlights the importance of hospitality and the possibility of encountering the divine in unexpected ways.

Responsorial Psalm: Psalms 15: 2-3ab, 3cd-4, 5

R. (1a) He who does justice will live in the presence of the Lord.

2 He that walketh without blemish, and worketh justice:

3ab He that speaketh truth in his heart, who hath not used deceit in his tongue.

R. He who does justice will live in the presence of the Lord.

3cd Nor hath done evil to his neighbour: nor taken up a reproach against his neighbours.

4 In his sight the malignant is brought to nothing: but he glorifieth them that fear the Lord.

R. He who does justice will live in the presence of the Lord.

5 He that hath not put out his money to usury, nor taken bribes against the innocent: He that doth these things shall not be moved for ever.

R. He who does justice will live in the presence of the Lord.

Mysteries Revealed Through Suffering (Colossians 1: 24-28):

24 Who now rejoice in my sufferings for you, and fill up those things that are wanting of the sufferings of Christ, in my flesh, for his body, which is the church:

25 Whereof I am made a minister according to the dispensation of God, which is given me towards you, that I may fulfill the word of God:

26 The mystery which hath been hidden from ages and generations, but now is manifested to his saints,

27 To whom God would make known the riches of the glory of this mystery among the Gentiles, which is Christ, in you the hope of glory.

28 Whom we preach, admonishing every man, and teaching every man in all wisdom, that we may present every man perfect in Christ Jesus.

The second reading from Colossians emphasizes Paul's willingness to suffer for the sake of the gospel. He sees his suffering as a way to fill up what is lacking in Christ's afflictions. This passage can be interpreted metaphorically, suggesting that we all have a role to play in sharing the gospel message, even if it involves challenges or sacrifices.

Alleluia: Luke 8: 15

R. Alleluia, alleluia.

15 Blessed are they who have kept the word with a generous heart and yield a harvest through perseverance.

R. Alleluia, alleluia.

The Better Part (Luke 10: 38-42):

38 Now it came to pass as they went, that he entered into a certain town: and a certain woman named Martha, received him into her house.

39 And she had a sister called Mary, who sitting also at the Lord's feet, heard his word.

40 But Martha was busy about much serving. Who stood and said: Lord, hast thou no care that my sister hath left me alone to serve? speak to her therefore, that she help me.

41 And the Lord answering, said to her: Martha, Martha, thou art careful, and art troubled about many things:

42 But one thing is necessary. Mary hath chosen the best part, which shall not be taken away from her.

The Gospel of Luke presents the story of Martha and Mary. Jesus visits their home, and Martha busies herself with preparing a meal, while Mary sits at Jesus' feet, listening to his teaching. Martha becomes frustrated and complains to Jesus about Mary's lack of help. Jesus gently rebukes Martha, saying that Mary has chosen "the better part," which will not be taken away from her. This passage highlights the importance of listening to God's word and choosing what is truly valuable over worldly distractions.

Reflect & Respond

- How does the story of Abraham in Genesis challenge you to consider how you treat guests or strangers?

- Consider Paul's message in Colossians. What does it mean to suffer for the sake of the gospel?

- The story of Martha and Mary is a reminder to prioritize our relationship with God. How can you create more space in your life for listening to God's voice?

Prayer

Dear God, grant us the gift of hospitality, that we may welcome others with open hearts and minds. Help us to discern your voice in the midst of life's distractions. May we choose the better part, focusing on what is truly important in your sight. Amen.

Challenge

This week, consider practicing hospitality by inviting someone over for a meal or simply offering a listening ear. Be mindful of opportunities to quiet your mind and listen for God's voice in prayer, scripture reading, or reflection. You can also reflect on your own priorities in life. Are you spending time on the things that truly matter, or are you getting caught up in distractions?

Notes:_____

_____

_____

_____

_____

_____

_____

_____

_____

_____

_____

_____

_____

Sunday, July 27

- Seventeenth Sunday in Ordinary Time

First Reading: Genesis 18: 20-32

Responsorial Psalm: Psalms 138: 1-2, 2-3, 6-7, 7-8

Second Reading: Colossians 2: 12-14

Alleluia: Romans 8: 15bc

Gospel: Luke 11: 1-13

Lectionary: 111

This week's readings focus on themes of persistence in prayer, faith, and God's enduring mercy.

Abraham Intercedes for Sodom (Genesis 18: 20-32):

20 And the Lord said: The cry of Sodom and Gomorrha is multiplied, and their sin is become exceedingly grievous.

21 I will go down and see whether they have done according to the cry that is come to me: or whether it be not so, that I may know.

22 And they turned themselves from thence, and went their way to Sodom: but Abraham as yet stood before the Lord.

23 And drawing nigh he said: Wilt thou destroy the just with the wicked?

24 If there be fifty just men in the city, shall they perish withal? and wilt thou not spare that place for the sake of the fifty just, if they be therein?

25 Far be it from thee to do this thing, and to slay the just with the wicked, and for the just to be in like case as the wicked, this is not beseeming thee: thou who judgest all the earth, wilt not make this judgment.

26 And the Lord said to him: If I find in Sodom fifty just within the city, I will spare the whole place for their sake.

27 And Abraham answered, and said: Seeing I have once begun, I will speak to my Lord, whereas I am dust and ashes.

28 What if there be five less than fifty just persons? wilt thou for five and forty destroy the whole city? And he said: I will not destroy it, if I find five and forty.

29 And again he said to him: But if forty be found there, what wilt thou do? He said: I will not destroy it for the sake of forty.

30 Lord, saith he, be not angry, I beseech thee, if I speak: What if thirty shall be found there? He answered: I will not do it, if I find thirty there.

31 Seeing, saith he, I have once begun, I will speak to my Lord. What if twenty be found there? He said: I will not destroy it for the sake of twenty.

32 I beseech thee, saith he, be not angry, Lord, if I speak yet once more: What if ten should be found there? And he said: I will not destroy it for the sake of ten.

The first reading from Genesis picks up on the story of Abraham's encounter with the divine visitors. The Lord reveals his intention to destroy Sodom and Gomorrah because of their wickedness. Abraham pleads for mercy, bargaining with God to spare the cities if there are righteous people living there. This passage highlights God's willingness to listen to our prayers and Abraham's faith in God's justice and mercy.

Responsorial Psalm: Psalms 138: 1-2, 2-3, 6-7, 7-8

R. (3a) Lord, on the day I called for help, you answered me.

1 I will praise thee, O lord, with my whole heart: for thou hast heard the words of my mouth. I will sing praise to thee in the sight of his angels:

2ab I will worship towards thy holy temple, and I will give glory to thy name.

R. Lord, on the day I called for help, you answered me.

2cd For thy mercy, and for thy truth: for thou hast magnified thy holy name above all.

3 In what day soever I shall call upon thee, hear me: thou shall multiply strength in my soul.

R. Lord, on the day I called for help, you answered me.

6 For the Lord is high, and looketh on the low: and the high he knoweth afar off.

7abc If I shall walk in the midst of tribulation, thou wilt quicken me: and thou hast stretched forth thy hand against the wrath of my enemies.

R. Lord, on the day I called for help, you answered me.

7d Thy right hand hath saved me.

8 The Lord will repay for me: thy mercy, O Lord, endureth for ever: O despise not the work of thy hands.

R. Lord, on the day I called for help, you answered me.

Freed from the Power of Darkness (Colossians 2: 12-14):

12 Buried with him in baptism, in whom also you are risen again by the faith of the operation of God, who hath raised him up from the dead.

13 And you, when you were dead in your sins, and the uncircumcision of your flesh; he hath quickened together with him, forgiving you all offences:

14 Blotting out the handwriting of the decree that was against us, which was contrary to us. And he hath taken the same out of the way, fastening it to the cross:

The second reading from Colossians emphasizes the transformative power of Christ's sacrifice. Through baptism, we are buried with Christ in death and raised with him in new life. We are freed from the power of darkness and reconciled to God. This passage highlights the gift of salvation through faith in Jesus Christ.

R. Alleluia, alleluia.

15bc You have received a Spirit of adoption, through which we cry, Abba, Father.

R. Alleluia, alleluia.

Ask, Seek, Knock (Luke 11: 1-13):

1 And it came to pass, that as he was in a certain place praying, when he ceased, one of his disciples said to him: Lord, teach us to pray, as John also taught his disciples.

2 And he said to them: When you pray, say: Father, hallowed be thy name. Thy kingdom come.

3 Give us this day our daily bread.

4 And forgive us our sins, for we also forgive every one that is indebted to us. And lead us not into temptation.

5 And he said to them: Which of you shall have a friend, and shall go to him at midnight, and shall say to him: Friend, lend me three loaves,

6 Because a friend of mine is come off his journey to me, and I have not what to set before him.

7 And he from within should answer, and say: Trouble me not, the door is now shut, and my children are with me in bed; I cannot rise and give thee.

8 Yet if he shall continue knocking, I say to you, although he will not rise and give him, because he is his friend; yet, because of his importunity, he will rise, and give him as many as he needeth.

9 And I say to you, Ask, and it shall be given you: seek, and you shall find: knock, and it shall be opened to you.

10 For every one that asketh, receiveth; and he that seeketh, findeth; and to him that knocketh, it shall be opened.

11 And which of you, if he ask his father bread, will he give him a stone? or a fish, will he for a fish give him a serpent?

12 Or if he shall ask an egg, will he reach him a scorpion?

13 If you then, being evil, know how to give good gifts to your children, how much more will your Father from heaven give the good Spirit to them that ask him?

The Gospel of Luke presents Jesus teaching his disciples

about prayer. He encourages them to be persistent in prayer, like a friend who goes to another friend in the middle of the night to ask for bread. Jesus assures them that God will give good gifts to those who ask. This passage highlights the importance of prayer and God's generous provision for his children.

Reflect & Respond

- How does the story of Abraham's intercession for Sodom challenge you to consider the power of prayer?

- Consider the message of Colossians about being freed from the power of darkness. How does this concept impact your understanding of salvation?

- The parable of persistent prayer encourages us to keep asking, seeking, and knocking. Is there something you have been praying for? Don't give up hope! Continue to trust in God's timing and faithfulness.

Prayer

Dear God, teach us to pray with persistence and faith. Thank you for your mercy and grace, which endure forever. May we live in the freedom you offer through Christ, our Lord. Amen.

Challenge

This week, dedicate some time to focused prayer. You can use a specific prayer method like journaling your prayers or creating a prayer list. Remember, prayer is simply a conversation with God. You can share your joys, sorrows, and petitions with him, knowing that he hears and cares for you. You can also reflect on areas in your life where you may feel trapped or bound by darkness. Seek

God's help and trust in his power
to set you free.

Notes:_____

_____
_____
_____
_____
_____
_____
_____
_____
_____
_____
_____
_____
_____
_____
_____
_____
_____
_____
_____
_____
_____
_____
_____
_____
_____
_____
_____
_____
_____
_____
_____
_____
_____
_____
_____
_____
_____
_____
_____
_____
_____

August 2025

Sunday, August 3

- Eighteenth Sunday in Ordinary Time

First Reading: Ecclesiastes 1: 2; 2: 21-23

Responsorial Psalm: Psalms 90: 3-4, 5-6, 12-13, 14 and 17

Second Reading: Colossians 3: 1-5, 9-11

Alleluia: Matthew 5: 3

Gospel: Luke 12: 13-21

Lectionary: 114

This week's readings focus on themes of finding meaning in life, setting our priorities on heavenly things, and avoiding the sin of greed.

The Vanity of Life (Ecclesiastes 1: 2; 2: 21-23):

2 Vanity of vanities, said Ecclesiastes vanity of vanities, and all is vanity.

2:21 For when a man laboureth in wisdom, and knowledge, and carefulness, he leaveth what he hath gotten to an idle man: so this also is vanity, and a great evil.

22 For what profit shall a man have of all his labour, and vexation of spirit, with which he hath been tormented under the sun?

23 All his days are full of sorrows and miseries, even in the night he doth not rest in mind: and is not this vanity?

The first reading from Ecclesiastes presents the Preacher's reflections on the fleeting nature of life and the futility of pursuing earthly pleasures and possessions. This passage can be a reminder to seek something more lasting than worldly pursuits.

R. (1) If today you hear his voice, harden not your hearts.

3 Turn not man away to be brought low: and thou hast said: Be converted, O ye sons of men.

4 For a thousand years in thy sight are as yesterday, which is past. And as a watch in the night,

R. If today you hear his voice, harden not your hearts.

5 Things that are counted nothing, shall their years be.

6 In the morning man shall grow up like grass; in the morning he shall flourish and pass away: in the evening he shall fall, grow dry, and wither.

R. If today you hear his voice, harden not your hearts.

12 Can number thy wrath? So make thy right hand known: and men learned in heart, in wisdom.

13 Return, O Lord, how long? and be entreated in favour of thy servants.

R. If today you hear his voice, harden not your hearts.

14 We are filled in the morning with thy mercy: and we have rejoiced, and are delighted all our days.

17 And let the brightness of the Lord our God be upon us: and direct thou the works of our hands over us; yea, the work of our hands do thou direct.

R. If today you hear his voice, harden not your hearts.

Set Your Hearts on Things Above (Colossians 3: 1-5, 9-11):

1 Therefore, if you be risen with Christ, seek the things that are above; where Christ is sitting at the right hand of God:

2 Mind the things that are above, not the things that are upon the earth.

3 For you are dead; and your life is hid with Christ in God.

4 When Christ shall appear, who is your life, then you also shall appear with him in glory.

5 Mortify therefore your members which are upon the earth; fornication, uncleanness, lust, evil concupiscence, and covetousness, which is the service of idols.

9 Lie not one to another: stripping yourselves of the old man with his deeds,

10 And putting on the new, him who is renewed unto knowledge, according to the image of him that created him.

11 Where there is neither Gentile nor Jew, circumcision nor uncircumcision, Barbarian nor Scythian, bond nor free. But Christ is all, and in all.

The second reading from Colossians encourages us to set our hearts on things above, where Christ is seated at the right hand of God. We are called to put to death earthly desires and live in a way that reflects our new identity in Christ. This passage emphasizes the importance of living for what truly matters in God's eyes.

Alleluia: Matthew 5: 3

R. Alleluia, alleluia.

3 Blessed are the poor in spirit, for theirs is the kingdom of heaven.

R. Alleluia, alleluia.

The Parable of the Rich Fool (Luke 12: 13-21):

13 And one of the multitude said to him: Master, speak to my brother that he divide the inheritance with me.

14 But he said to him: Man, who hath appointed me judge, or divider, over you?

15 And he said to them: Take heed and beware of all covetousness; for a man's life doth not consist in the abundance of things which he possesseth.

16 And he spoke a similitude to them, saying: The land of a certain rich man brought forth plenty of fruits.

17 And he thought within himself, saying: What shall I do, because I have no room where to bestow my fruits?

18 And he said: This will I do: I will pull down my barns, and will build greater; and into them will I gather all things that are grown to me, and my goods.

19 And I will say to my soul: Soul, thou hast much goods laid up for many years take thy rest; eat, drink, make good cheer.

20 But God said to him: Thou fool, this night do they require thy soul of thee: and whose shall those things be which thou hast provided?

21 So is he that layeth up treasure for himself, and is not rich towards God.

The Gospel of Luke presents the Parable of the Rich Fool. A man worries about having enough possessions because his crops have yielded abundantly. He plans to tear down his barns and build bigger ones to store his wealth. However, God calls him a fool, reminding him that his life could be over that very night. This passage serves as a warning against greed and the importance of storing up treasures in heaven.

Reflect & Respond

- How does the reading from Ecclesiastes challenge you to consider what truly matters in life?

- Consider the message of Colossians about setting our hearts on things above. What practical steps can you take to focus more on heavenly things?

- The Parable of the Rich Fool is a cautionary tale. How can you avoid the sin of greed in your own life?

Prayer

Dear God, help us to see through the fleeting pleasures of this world and set our hearts on things that are eternal. Grant us the wisdom to use our possessions wisely and to store up treasures in heaven, where true riches lie. Amen.

Challenge

This week, take some time to reflect on your own values and priorities. What are you spending your time and energy on? Is there a shift you need to make to live a more Christ-centered life? Consider simplifying your life or practicing generosity by giving to those in need. You can also explore resources about Christian stewardship, which is the practice of managing your resources wisely according to God's principles.

Notes:_____
_____
_____
_____
_____
_____
_____
_____
_____
_____
_____

Sunday, August 10

- Nineteenth Sunday in Ordinary Time

First Reading: Wisdom 18: 6-9

Responsorial Psalm: Psalms 33: 1, 12, 18-19, 20-22

Second Reading: Hebrews 11: 1-2, 8-19 or 11: 1-2, 8-12

Alleluia: Matthew 24: 42a, 44

Gospel: Luke 12: 32-48

Lectionary: 117

This Sunday's readings invite us to loosen our grip on anxieties and embrace a life of trust in God's providence. We'll encounter stories of unwavering faith, practical advice for overcoming worry, and a powerful reminder to keep our focus on what truly matters.

God's Faithful Protection (Wisdom 18: 6-9):

6 For that night was known before by our fathers, that assuredly knowing what oaths they had trusted to, they might be of better courage.

7 So thy people received the salvation of the just, and destruction of the unjust.

8 For as thou didst punish the adversaries: so thou didst also encourage and glorify us.

9 For the just children of good men were offering sacrifice secretly, and they unanimously ordered a law of justice: that the just should receive both good and evil alike, singing now the praises of the fathers.

The Book of Wisdom opens the service with a story that highlights God's unwavering faithfulness. Even in the midst of darkness, as with the Israelites' escape from Egypt, God protects his people. This passage assures us that we can trust in His presence and care, even when we face challenges.

Responsorial Psalm: Psalms 33: 1, 12, 18-19, 20-22

R. (12b) Blessed the people the Lord has chosen to be his own.

1 Rejoice in the Lord, O ye just: praise becometh the upright.

12 Blessed is the nation whose God is the Lord: the people whom he hath chosen for his inheritance.

R. Blessed the people the Lord has chosen to be his own.

18 Behold the eyes of the Lord are on them that fear him: and on them that hope in his mercy.

19 To deliver their souls from death; and feed them in famine.

R. Blessed the people the Lord has chosen to be his own.

20 Our soul waiteth for the Lord: for he is our helper and protector.

21 For in him our heart shall rejoice: and in his holy name we have trusted.

22 Let thy mercy, O Lord, be upon us, as we have hoped in thee.

R. Blessed the people the Lord has chosen to be his own.

Heroes of Faith (Hebrews 11: 1-2, 8-19 or 11: 1-2, 8-12):

1 Now faith is the substance of things to be hoped for, the evidence of things that appear not.

2 For by this the ancients obtained a testimony.

8 By faith he that is called Abraham, obeyed to go out into a place which he was to receive for an inheritance; and he went out, not knowing whither he went.

9 By faith he abode in the land, dwelling in cottages, with Isaac and Jacob, the co-heirs of the same promise.

10 For he looked for a city that hath foundations; whose builder and maker is God.

11 By faith also Sara herself, being barren, received strength to conceive seed, even past the time of age; because she believed that he was faithful who had promised,

12 For which cause there sprung even from one (and him as good as dead) as the stars of heaven in multitude, and as the sand which is by the sea shore innumerable.

13 All these died according to faith, not having received the promises, but beholding them afar off, and saluting them, and confessing that they are pilgrims and strangers on the earth.

14 For they that say these things, do signify that they seek a country.

15 And truly if they had been mindful of that from whence they came out, they had doubtless time to return.

16 But now they desire a better, that is to say, a heavenly country. Therefore God is not ashamed to be called their God; for he hath prepared for them a city.

17 By faith Abraham, when he was tried, offered Isaac: and he that had received the promises, offered up his only begotten son;

18 (To whom it was said: In Isaac shall thy seed be called.)

19 Accounting that God is able to raise up even from the dead. Whereupon also he received him for a parable.

Or

1 Now faith is the substance of things to be hoped for, the evidence of things that appear not.

2 For by this the ancients obtained a testimony.

8 By faith he that is called Abraham, obeyed to go out into a place which he was to receive for an inheritance; and he went out, not knowing whither he went.

9 By faith he abode in the land, dwelling in cottages, with Isaac and Jacob, the co-heirs of the same promise.

10 For he looked for a city that hath foundations; whose builder and maker is God.

11 By faith also Sara herself, being barren, received strength to conceive seed, even past the time of age; because she believed that he was faithful who had promised,

12 For which cause there sprung even from one (and him as good as dead) as the stars of heaven in multitude, and as the sand which is by the sea shore innumerable.

The Letter to the Hebrews presents a remarkable cast of characters – men and women like Abraham and Sarah who lived lives marked by extraordinary faith. Despite uncertainties, they trusted in God's promises. Their stories serve as an inspiration for us to develop our own unwavering faith.

Alleluia: Matthew 24: 42a, 44

R. Alleluia, alleluia.

42a, 44 Stay awake and be ready! For you do not know on what day your Lord will come.

R. Alleluia, alleluia.

Letting Go of Anxiety (Luke 12: 32-48):

32 Fear not, little flock, for it hath pleased your Father to give you a kingdom.

33 Sell what you possess and give alms. Make to yourselves bags which grow not old, a treasure in heaven which faileth not: where no thief approacheth, nor moth corrupteth.

34 For where your treasure is, there will your heart be also.

35 Let your loins be girt, and lamps burning in your hands.

36 And you yourselves like to men who wait for their lord, when he shall return from the wedding; that when he cometh and knocketh, they may open to him immediately.

37 Blessed are those servants, whom the Lord when he cometh, shall find watching. Amen I say to you, that he will gird himself, and make them sit down to meat, and passing will minister unto them.

38 And if he shall come in the second watch, or come in the third watch, and find them so, blessed are those servants.

39 But this know ye, that if the householder did know at what hour the thief would come, he would surely watch, and would not suffer his house to be broken open.

40 Be you then also ready: for at what hour you think not, the Son of man will come.

41 And Peter said to him: Lord, dost thou speak this parable to us, or likewise to all?

42 And the Lord said: Who (thinkest thou) is the faithful and wise steward, whom his lord setteth over his family, to give them their measure of wheat in due season?

43 Blessed is that servant, whom when his lord shall come, he shall find so doing.

44 Verily I say to you, he will set him over all that he possesseth.

45 But if that servant shall say in his heart: My lord is long a coming; and shall begin to strike the menservants and maidservants, and to eat and to drink and be drunk:

46 The lord of that servant will come in the day that he hopeth not, and at the hour that he knoweth not, and shall separate him, and shall appoint him his portion with unbelievers.

47 And that servant who knew the will of his lord, and prepared not himself, and did not according to his will, shall be beaten with many stripes.

48 But he that knew not, and did things worthy of stripes, shall be beaten with few stripes. And unto whomsoever much is given, of him much shall be required: and to whom they have committed much, of him they will demand the more.

In the Gospel of Luke, Jesus offers practical guidance for overcoming worry. He encourages us to look at the birds and the flowers – God takes care of them, and surely He cares for us even more! By prioritizing God's kingdom and righteousness, we can release our anxieties and live with a lighter heart.

Reflect and Respond:

- Can you recall a time in your life when you experienced God's faithfulness, even during a difficult situation?

- Think about the heroes of faith mentioned in Hebrews. Is there a particular person whose story resonates with you? Why?

- What are some practical ways you can incorporate Jesus' teachings on letting go of worry into your daily life?

A Prayer for Peace:

Dear God, grant us the unwavering faith of the heroes we encounter in Scripture. Help us to trust in your promises and overcome our anxieties. May we focus on your kingdom and righteousness, and experience the freedom that comes from letting go of worry. Amen.

Living with Less Worry:

- This week, choose a specific worry that has been weighing on you. Write it down, then pray and ask God to replace your anxiety with trust in His plan.

- Practice gratitude! Take a moment each day to appreciate the beauty and abundance in your life, recognizing God's provision.

- Can you think of someone who might be struggling with worry? Reach out and offer them a listening ear and words of encouragement. Remember, we are all on this faith journey together!

Notes:_____
_____
_____
_____
_____
_____
_____
_____
_____
_____
_____
_____
_____
_____
_____
_____
_____
_____
_____
_____
_____
_____
_____
_____

Sunday, August 17

- Twentieth Sunday in Ordinary Time

First Reading: Jeremiah 38: 4-6, 8-10

Responsorial Psalm: Psalms 40: 2, 3, 4, 18

Second Reading: Hebrews 12: 1-4

Alleluia: John 10: 27

Gospel: Luke 12: 49-53

Lectionary: 120

This Sunday's readings explore themes of courage, perseverance, and the transformative power of faith. We'll encounter a story of dramatic rescue, a call to stay the course, and a powerful image of Jesus bringing division, but for a purpose.

A Daring Rescue (Jeremiah 38: 4-6, 8-10):

4 And the princes said to the king: We beseech thee that this man may be put to death: for on purpose he weakeneth the hands of the men of war, that remain in this city, and the hands of the people, speaking to them according to these words: for this man seeketh not peace to this people, but evil.

5 And king Sedecias said: Behold he is in your hands: for it is not lawful for the king to deny you any thing.

6 Then they took Jeremias and cast him into the dungeon of Melchias the son of Amelech, which was in the entry of the prison: and they let down Jeremias by ropes into the dungeon, wherein there was no water, but mire. And Jeremias sunk into the mire.

8 And Abdemelech went out of the king's house, and spoke to the king, saying:

9 My lord the king, these men have done evil in all that they have done against Jeremias the prophet, casting him into the dungeon to die there with hunger, for there is no more bread in the city.

10 Then the king commanded Abdemelech the Ethiopian, saying: Take from hence thirty men with thee, and draw up Jeremias the prophet out of the dungeon, before he die.

The Book of Jeremiah opens the service with a story of perseverance. Jeremiah, thrown into a cistern for his prophecies, is rescued by an Ethiopian eunuch named Ebed-Melech. This dramatic act of courage highlights the importance of standing up for what is right, even in the face of danger.

Responsorial Psalm: Psalms 40: 2, 3, 4, 18

R. (14b) Lord, come to my aid!

2 With expectation I have waited for the Lord, and he was attentive to me.

R. Lord, come to my aid!

3 And he heard my prayers, and brought me out of the pit of misery and the mire of dregs. And he set my feet upon a rock, and directed my steps.

R. Lord, come to my aid!

4 And he put a new canticle into my mouth, a song to our God. Many shall see, and shall fear: and they shall hope in the Lord.

R. Lord, come to my aid!

18 But I am a beggar and poor: the Lord is careful for me. Thou art my helper and my protector: O my God, be not slack.

R. Lord, come to my aid!

Running the Race (Hebrews 12: 1-4):

1 And therefore we also having so great a cloud of witnesses over our head, laying aside every weight and sin which surrounds us, let us run by patience to the fight proposed to us:

2 Looking on Jesus, the author and finisher of faith, who having joy set before him, endured the cross, despising the shame, and now sitteth on the right hand of the throne of God.

3 For think diligently upon him that endured such opposition from sinners against himself; that you be not wearied, fainting in your minds.

4 For you have not yet resisted unto blood, striving against sin:

The Letter to the Hebrews uses the metaphor of a race to encourage us in our faith journeys. We are surrounded by a "great cloud of witnesses" – those who have come before us in faith. The passage reminds us to stay focused on Jesus, the source of our strength, and to persevere through challenges.

Alleluia: John 10: 27

R. Alleluia, alleluia.

27 My sheep hear my voice, says the Lord; I know them, and they follow me.

R. Alleluia, alleluia.

Fire and Division (Luke 12: 49-53):

49 I am come to cast fire on the earth; and what will I, but that it be kindled?

50 And I have a baptism wherewith I am to be baptized: and how am I straitened until it be accomplished?

51 Think ye, that I am come to give peace on earth? I tell you, no; but separation.

52 For there shall be from henceforth five in one house divided: three against two, and two against three.

53 The father shall be divided against the son, and the son against his father, the mother against the daughter, and the daughter against the mother, the mother in law against her daughter in law, and the daughter in law against her mother in law.

In the Gospel of Luke, Jesus presents a seemingly discordant image: He declares that he has come to bring fire upon the earth. This fire represents the transformative power of faith, which can sometimes cause division as people choose to follow Jesus or not. Ultimately, Jesus emphasizes the importance of embracing his teachings, even if it leads to discomfort or change.

Reflect and Respond:

- Can you think of a time when you had to take a courageous stand for your beliefs?

- How can the image of the "great cloud of witnesses" from Hebrews encourage you in your faith journey?

- Jesus' message of bringing fire can be interpreted as a call for change. Is there an area of your life where you might need to embrace change or challenge the status quo?

A Prayer for Strength:

Dear God, grant us the courage to stand up for what is right, even when it's difficult. Help us to persevere in our faith journeys, keeping our eyes fixed on you. May we be open to the transformative power of your word, even if it brings challenges or change. Amen.

Living with Fire (embracing transformation):

- This week, reflect on an area of your life where you might be feeling stuck or stagnant. Pray for the courage to embrace change and ask God to guide you towards growth and transformation.

- The "cloud of witnesses" mentioned in Hebrews includes many inspiring figures. Spend some time researching these figures and learning about their lives. How can their stories inspire your own faith journey?

- Think about someone you know who might be struggling with their faith. Offer them words of encouragement and support, reminding them that they are not alone on this path.

Notes:_____

Sunday, August 24

- Twenty-first Sunday in Ordinary Time

First Reading: Isaiah 66: 18-21

Responsorial Psalm: Psalms 117: 1, 2

Second Reading: Hebrews 12: 5-7, 11-13

Alleluia: John 14: 6

Gospel: Luke 13: 22-30

Lectionary: 123

This Sunday's readings delve into themes of patience, perseverance, and the importance of not giving up on the path towards God. We'll encounter a message of universal inclusion, a reminder to endure trials, and a parable that challenges us to strive for the narrow gate.

Gathering All Nations (Isaiah 66: 18-21):

18 But I know their works, and their thoughts: I come that I may gather them together with all nations and tongues: and they shall come and shall see my glory.

19 And I will set a sign among them, and I will send of them that shall be saved, to the Gentiles into the sea, into Africa, and Lydia them that draw the bow: into Italy, and Greece, to the islands afar off, to them that have not heard of me, and have not seen my glory. And they shall declare my glory to the Gentiles:

20 And they shall bring all your brethren out of all nations for a gift to the Lord, upon horses, and in chariots, and in litters, and on mules, and in coaches, to my holy mountain Jerusalem, saith the Lord, as if the children of Israel should bring an offering in a clean vessel into the house of the Lord.

21 And I will take of them to be priests, and Levites, saith the Lord.

The Book of Isaiah opens the service with a message of hope

and inclusivity. God desires to gather all nations and people from the farthest corners of the earth. This passage reminds us that God's love extends to everyone, regardless of background or belief.

R. (Mk 16:15) Go out to all the world and tell the Good News.

Or R. Alleluia.

1 O praise the Lord, all ye nations: praise him, all ye people.

R. Go out to all the world and tell the Good News.

Or R. Alleluia.

2 For his mercy is confirmed upon us: and the truth of the Lord remaineth for ever.

R. Go out to all the world and tell the Good News.

or

R. Alleluia.

Enduring Trials (Hebrews 12: 5-7, 11-13):

5 And you have forgotten the consolation, which speaketh to you, as unto children, saying: My son, neglect not the discipline of the Lord; neither be thou wearied whilst thou art rebuked by him.

6 For whom the Lord loveth, he chastiseth; and he scourgeth every son whom he receiveth.

7 Persevere under discipline. God dealeth with you as with his sons; for what son is there, whom the father doth not correct?

11 Now all chastisement for the present indeed seemeth not to bring with it joy, but sorrow: but afterwards it will yield, to them that are exercised by it, the most peaceable fruit of justice.

12 Wherefore lift up the hands which hang down, and the feeble knees,

13 And make straight steps with your feet: that no one, halting, may go out of the way: but rather be healed.

The Letter to the Hebrews continues the theme of perseverance. The author uses the metaphor of God's discipline as a loving parent to encourage us to endure trials. These challenges are not meant to punish us, but to help us grow stronger in our faith.

Alleluia: John 14: 6

R. Alleluia, alleluia.

6 I am the way, the truth and the life, says the Lord; no one comes to the Father, except through me.

R. Alleluia, alleluia.

The Narrow Gate (Luke 13: 22-30):

22 And he went through the cities and towns teaching, and making his journey to Jerusalem.

23 And a certain man said to him: Lord, are they few that are saved? But he said to them:

24 Strive to enter by the narrow gate; for many, I say to you, shall seek to enter, and shall not be able.

25 But when the master of the house shall be gone in, and shall shut the door, you shall begin to stand without, and knock at the door, saying: Lord, open to us. And he answering, shall say to you: I know you not, whence you are.

26 Then you shall begin to say: We have eaten and drunk in thy presence, and thou hast taught in our streets.

27 And he shall say to you: I know you not, whence you are: depart from me, all ye workers of iniquity.

28 There shall be weeping and gnashing of teeth, when you shall see Abraham and Isaac and Jacob, and all the prophets, in the kingdom of God, and you yourselves thrust out.

29 And there shall come from the east and the west, and the north and the south; and shall sit down in the kingdom of God.

30 And behold, they are last that shall be first; and they are first that shall be last.

The Gospel of Luke presents the parable of the narrow gate. Jesus emphasizes the importance of striving to enter the kingdom of God, even if the way is difficult. The parable reminds us that not everyone will be able to enter, but it also offers a message of hope – those who are persistent and seek God with all their hearts will find a place at his table.

Reflect and Respond:

- How can you be more inclusive and welcoming towards others in your daily life?

- Can you think of a time in your life when you had to endure a challenge? How did your faith help you persevere?

- The parable of the narrow gate can be interpreted as a call to action. What steps can you take to be more intentional about growing closer to God?

A Prayer for Perseverance:

Dear God, grant us the patience and perseverance to endure the trials we face in life. Help us to see these challenges as opportunities for growth and to draw closer to you. May we strive to enter your kingdom with all our hearts. Amen.

Living with Purpose:

- This week, reflect on your own values and goals. Are they aligned with your faith? If not, consider making some changes to live a more purposeful life that reflects your commitment to God.

- The parable mentions many trying to enter the gate but failing. Can you think of someone who might be struggling on their faith journey? Offer them support and encouragement, reminding them that God's love is always available.

- Spend some time in prayer or meditation this week. Focus on quieting your mind and listening for God's voice in your life.

Notes:_____

Sunday, August 31

- Twenty-second Sunday in Ordinary Time

First Reading: Sirach 3: 17-18, 20, 28-29

Responsorial Psalm: Psalms 68: 4-5, 6-7, 10-11

Second Reading: Hebrews 12: 18-19, 22-24

Alleluia: Matthew 11: 29ab

Gospel: Luke 14: 1, 7-14

Lectionary: 126

This Sunday's readings weave a tapestry of humility, hospitality, and seeking the right perspective. We'll encounter wise advice on proper conduct, a reminder of the heavenly banquet awaiting us, and a parable that challenges our assumptions about seeking recognition.

The Wisdom of Humility (Sirach 3: 17-18, 20, 28-29):

17 My son, do thy works in meekness, and thou shalt be beloved above the glory of men.

18 The greater thou art, the more humble thyself in all things, and thou shalt find grace before God:

20 Seek not the things that are too high for thee, and search not into things above thy ability: but the things that God hath commanded thee, think on them always, and in many of his works be not curious.

28 The heart of the wise is understood in wisdom, and a good ear will hear wisdom with all desire. A wise heart, and which hath understanding, will abstain from sins, and in the works of justice shall have success.

29 Water quencheth a flaming fire, and alms resisteth sins:

The Book of Sirach opens the service with practical wisdom. The passage emphasizes the importance of humility and

217

respecting those in authority. It reminds us that true greatness comes not from seeking attention, but from living a life of integrity and honoring God.

Responsorial Psalm: Psalms 68: 4-5, 6-7, 10-11

R. (11b) God, in your goodness, you have made a home for the poor.

4 Let the just feast, and rejoice before God: and be delighted with gladness.

5 Sing ye to God, sing a psalm to his name, make a way for him who ascendeth upon the west: the Lord is his name. Rejoice ye before him: but the wicked shall be troubled at his presence,

R. God, in your goodness, you have made a home for the poor.

6 Who is the father of orphans, and the judge of widows. God in his holy place:

7 God who maketh men of one manner to dwell in a house: Who

bringeth out them that were bound in strength; in like manner them that provoke, that dwell in sepulchres.

R. God, in your goodness, you have made a home for the poor.

10 Thou shalt set aside for thy inheritance a free rain, O God: and it was weakened, but thou hast made it perfect.

11 In it shall thy animals dwell; in thy sweetness, O God, thou hast provided for the poor.

R. God, in your goodness, you have made a home for the poor.

The Heavenly Banquet (Hebrews 12: 18-19, 22-24):

18 For you are not come to a mountain that might be touched, and a burning fire, and a whirlwind, and darkness, and storm,

19 And the sound of a trumpet, and the voice of words, which they that heard excused themselves, that the word might not be spoken to them:

22 But you are come to mount Sion, and to the city of the living God, the heavenly Jerusalem, and to the company of many thousands of angels,

23 And to the church of the firstborn, who are written in the heavens, and to God the judge of all, and to the spirits of the just made perfect,

24 And to Jesus the mediator of the new testament, and to the sprinkling of blood which speaketh better than that of Abel.

The Letter to the Hebrews shifts our focus to the glorious future that awaits believers. The author uses the imagery of a heavenly assembly and Mount Zion to describe the joy and fellowship that will be ours in God's presence. This passage serves as a reminder of the ultimate reward for those who remain faithful.

Alleluia: Matthew 11: 29ab

R. Alleluia, alleluia.

29ab Take my yoke upon you, says the Lord, and learn from me, for I am meek and humble of heart.

R. Alleluia, alleluia.

Seeking the Lowest Place (Luke 14: 1, 7-14):

1 And it came to pass, when Jesus went into the house of one of the chief of the Pharisees, on the sabbath day, to eat bread, that they watched him.

7 And he spoke a parable also to them that were invited, marking how they chose the first seats at the table, saying to them:

8 When thou art invited to a wedding, sit not down in the first place, lest perhaps one more honourable than thou be invited by him:

9 And he that invited thee and him, come and say to thee, Give this man place: and then thou begin with shame to take the lowest place.

10 But when thou art invited, go, sit down in the lowest place; that when he who invited thee, cometh, he may say to thee: Friend, go up higher. Then shalt thou have glory before them that sit at table with thee.

11 Because every one that exalteth himself, shall be humbled; and he that humbleth himself, shall be exalted.

12 And he said to him also that had invited him: When thou makest a dinner or a supper, call not thy friends, nor thy brethren, nor thy kinsmen, nor thy neighbours who are rich; lest perhaps they also invite thee again, and a recompense be made to thee.

13 But when thou makest a feast, call the poor, the maimed, the lame, and the blind;

14 And thou shalt be blessed, because they have not wherewith to make thee recompense: for recompense shall be made thee at the resurrection of the just.

The Gospel of Luke presents the parable of the wedding feast. Jesus observes guests jockeying for the best seats and offers a counterintuitive message: seek the lowest place, for true honor comes from God. This parable challenges our pride and reminds us that humility is a core Christian value.

Reflect and Respond:

- How can you cultivate a more humble attitude in your daily interactions with others?

- The idea of a heavenly banquet is a powerful image. What does it evoke in you?

- The parable challenges us to avoid seeking the praise of others. Can you think of a situation where you might need to practice this teaching?

A Prayer for Humility:

Dear God, help us to walk in humility, seeking your approval above the praise of others. May we extend hospitality to those around us, reflecting your love and generosity. Prepare our hearts for the heavenly banquet that awaits us in your presence. Amen.

Living with Humility and Hospitality:

- This week, consider reaching out to someone you might not normally talk to or who might be feeling excluded. A simple act of kindness can go a long way.

- Spend some time reflecting on your own relationship with God. Are there areas where you might need to cultivate a greater sense of humility and dependence on Him?

- Is there someone in your life who could benefit from your hospitality? Invite them for a meal, offer to help them with a task, or simply lend a listening ear. Remember, hospitality is about opening our hearts and homes to others.

Notes:_____
_____
_____

221

September 2025

Sunday, September 7

- Twenty-third Sunday in Ordinary Time

First Reading: Wisdom 9: 13-18b

Responsorial Psalm: Psalms 90: 3-4, 5-6, 12-13, 14 and 17

Second Reading: Philemon 1: 9-10, 12-17

Alleluia: Psalms 119: 135

Gospel: Luke 14: 25-33

Lectionary: 129

This Sunday's readings delve into themes of commitment, sacrifice, and counting the cost of following Jesus.

We'll encounter a reflection on the value of divine wisdom, a story of reconciliation and grace, and a parable that challenges us to consider the true cost of discipleship.

The Value of Wisdom (Wisdom 9: 13-18b):

13 For who among men is he that can know the counsel of God? or who can think what the will of God is?

14 For the thoughts of mortal men are fearful, and our counsels uncertain.

15 For the corruptible body is a load upon the soul, and the earthly habitation presseth down the mind that museth upon many things.

16 And hardly do we guess aright at things that are upon earth: and with labour do we find the things that are before us. But the things that are in heaven, who shall search out?

17 And who shall know thy thought, except thou give wisdom, and send thy Holy Spirit from above:

18b And so the ways of them that are upon earth may be corrected.

The Book of Wisdom opens the service with a beautiful passage praising the power and importance of divine wisdom. This wisdom is described as all-encompassing, reaching from the highest heavens to the depths of human understanding. The passage reminds us that seeking God's wisdom is essential for living a fulfilling life.

Responsorial Psalm: Psalms 90: 3-4, 5-6, 12-13, 14 and 17

R. (1) In every age, O Lord, you have been our refuge.

3 Turn not man away to be brought low: and thou hast said: Be converted, O ye sons of men.

4 For a thousand years in thy sight are as yesterday, which is past. And as a watch in the night,

R. In every age, O Lord, you have been our refuge.

5 Things that are counted nothing, shall their years be.

6 In the morning man shall grow up like grass; in the morning he shall flourish and pass away: in the evening he shall fall, grow dry, and wither.

R. In every age, O Lord, you have been our refuge.

12 Can number thy wrath? So make thy right hand known: and men learned in heart, in wisdom.

13 Return, O Lord, how long? and be entreated in favour of thy servants.

R. In every age, O Lord, you have been our refuge.

14 We are filled in the morning with thy mercy: and we have rejoiced, and are delighted all our days.

17 And let the brightness of the Lord our God be upon us: and direct thou the works of our hands over us; yea, the work of our hands do thou direct.

R. In every age, O Lord, you have been our refuge.

Reconciliation and Grace (Philemon 1: 9-10, 12-17):

9 For charity sake I rather beseech, whereas thou art such a one, as Paul an old man, and now a prisoner also of Jesus Christ.

10 I beseech thee for my son, whom I have begotten in my bands, Onesimus,

12 Whom I have sent back to thee. And do thou receive him as my own bowels.

13 Whom I would have retained with me, that in thy stead he might have ministered to me in the bands of the gospel:

14 But without thy counsel I would do nothing: that thy good deed might not be as it were of necessity, but voluntary.

15 For perhaps he therefore departed for a season from thee, that thou mightest receive him again for ever:

16 Not now as a servant, but instead of a servant, a most dear brother, especially to me: but how much more to thee both in the flesh and in the Lord?

17 If therefore thou count me a partner, receive him as myself.

The Letter to Philemon offers a heartwarming story of forgiveness and reconciliation. Paul appeals to Philemon to welcome back his runaway slave, Onesimus, not as a slave, but as a beloved brother in Christ. This passage highlights the power of God's grace to heal relationships and foster forgiveness.

Alleluia: Psalms 119: 135

R. Alleluia, alleluia.

135 Let your face shine upon your servant; and teach me your laws.

R. Alleluia, alleluia.

Counting the Cost (Luke 14: 25-33):

25 And there went great multitudes with him. And turning, he said to them:

26 If any man come to me, and hate not his father, and mother, and wife, and children, and brethren, and sisters, yea and his own life also, he cannot be my disciple.

27 And whosoever doth not carry his cross and come after me, cannot be my disciple.

28 For which of you having a mind to build a tower, doth not first sit down, and reckon the charges that are necessary, whether he have wherewithal to finish it:

29 Lest, after he hath laid the foundation, and is not able to finish it, all that see it begin to mock him,

30 Saying: This man began to build, and was not able to finish.

31 Or what king, about to go to make war against another king, doth not first sit down, and think whether he be able, with ten thousand, to meet him that, with twenty thousand, cometh against him?

32 Or else, whilst the other is yet afar off, sending an embassy, he desireth conditions of peace.

33 So likewise every one of you that doth not renounce all that he possesseth, cannot be my disciple.

The Gospel of Luke presents the parable of the great banquet. Jesus warns potential disciples to consider the cost of following him. Just as a builder would count the cost before starting a project, we must be prepared to make sacrifices and prioritize our commitment to Christ. The parable reminds us that true discipleship requires dedication and a willingness to put our faith above all else.

Reflect and Respond:

- How can you actively seek God's wisdom in your daily life?

- Can you think of a situation where forgiveness or reconciliation might be needed?

- The parable of counting the cost is a challenge. What are some things you might need to sacrifice in order to follow Jesus more closely?

A Prayer for Commitment:

Dear God, grant us the wisdom to seek you above all else. Help us to extend forgiveness and reconciliation in our relationships, reflecting your boundless grace. May we count the cost of following you and be willing to make the necessary sacrifices to be your true disciples. Amen.

Living with Commitment:

- This week, spend some time in prayer or meditation, reflecting on your commitment to God. Are there areas where you feel you could be growing closer to him?

- Think about someone you might need to forgive or reach out to in reconciliation. Take a step towards healing that relationship this week.

- Consider your priorities in life. Is there anything that might be getting in the way of your commitment to God? Make adjustments as needed to ensure that your

faith remains at the center of your life.

Notes:_____
_____
_____
_____
_____
_____
_____
_____
_____
_____
_____
_____
_____
_____
_____
_____
_____
_____
_____
_____
_____
_____
_____
_____
_____
_____
_____

Sunday, September 14

- Triumph of the Holy Cross - Feast

First Reading: Numbers 21: 4b-9

Responsorial Psalm: Psalms 78: 1bc-2, 34-35, 36-37, 38

Second Reading: Philippians 2: 6-11

Gospel: John 3: 13-17

Lectionary: 638

This Sunday marks a special day in the Christian calendar – the Feast of the Triumph of the Holy Cross, also known as the Exaltation of the Cross. Today's readings offer a powerful message about sacrifice, salvation, and the enduring love of God.

A Sign of Hope (Numbers 21: 4b-9):

4b With the people began to be weary of their journey and labour:

5 And speaking against God and Moses, they said: Why didst thou bring us out of Egypt, to die in the wilderness? There is no bread, nor have we any waters: our soul now loatheth this very light food.

6 Wherefore the Lord sent among the people fiery serpents, which bit them and killed many of them.

7 Upon which they came to Moses, and said: We have sinned, because we have spoken against the Lord and thee: pray that he may take away these serpents from us. And Moses prayed for the people.

8 And the Lord said to him: Make brazen serpent, and set it up for a sign: whosoever being struck shall look on it, shall live.

9 Moses therefore made a brazen serpent, and set it up for a sign: which when they that were bitten looked upon, they were healed.

The first reading from the Book of Numbers recounts the story of the Israelites being bitten by poisonous snakes in the desert. Moses, following God's instructions, creates a bronze serpent mounted on a pole. Those who looked upon the serpent were healed. This foreshadows the saving power of the cross, where Jesus' sacrifice offers healing and redemption for all who believe.

Responsorial Psalm: Psalms 78: 1bc-2, 34-35, 36-37, 38

R. (7b) Do not forget the works of the Lord!

1 Attend, O my people, to my law: incline your ears to the words of my mouth.

2 I will open my mouth in parables: I will utter propositions from the beginning.

R. Do not forget the works of the Lord!

34 When he slew them, then they sought him: and they returned, and came to him early in the morning.

35 And they remembered that God was their helper: and the most high God their redeemer.

R. Do not forget the works of the Lord!

36 And they loved him with their mouth: and with their tongue they lied unto him:

37 But their heart was not right with him: nor were they counted faithful in his covenant.

R. Do not forget the works of the Lord!

38 But he is merciful, and will forgive their sins: and will not destroy them. And many a time did he turn away his anger: and did not kindle all his wrath.

R. Do not forget the works of the Lord!

Humility and Exaltation (Philippians 2: 6-11):

6 Who being in the form of God, thought it not robbery to be equal with God:

7 But emptied himself, taking the form of a servant, being made in the likeness of men, and in habit found as a man.

8 He humbled himself, becoming obedient unto death, even to the death of the cross.

9 For which cause God also hath exalted him, and hath given him a name which is above all names:

10 That in the name of Jesus every knee should bow, of those that are in heaven, on earth, and under the earth:

11 And that every tongue should confess that the Lord Jesus Christ is in the glory of God the Father.

The Letter to the Philippians presents a beautiful hymn about Christ's humility and sacrifice. Though He was equal to God, Jesus emptied Himself, taking on human form and enduring death on a cross. This act of obedience and love is the foundation of our salvation. God has exalted Jesus, giving Him the name above all names.

Alleluia

R. Alleluia, alleluia.

We adore you, O Christ, and we bless you, because by your Cross you have redeemed the world.

R. Alleluia, alleluia.

God's Love Revealed (John 3: 13-17):

13 And no man hath ascended into heaven, but he that descended from heaven, the Son of man who is in heaven.

14 And as Moses lifted up the serpent in the desert, so must the Son of man be lifted up:

15 That whosoever believeth in him, may not perish; but may have life everlasting.

16 For God so loved the world, as to give his only begotten Son; that whosoever believeth in him, may not perish, but may have life everlasting.

17 For God sent not his Son into the world, to judge the world, but that the world may be saved by him.

The Gospel of John presents a profound message about God's love for humanity. Just as Moses lifted up the serpent in the desert, so is the Son of Man lifted up – not to condemn the world, but to offer salvation to all who believe. This passage emphasizes the central role of the cross in God's plan of redemption.

Reflect and Respond:

- How does the story of the bronze serpent connect to the symbolism of the cross?

- Philippians describes Jesus' humility. Can you think of times in your life where showing humility has led to a positive outcome?

- The cross represents God's love and sacrifice for humanity. How can you share this message of hope with others?

A Prayer of Gratitude:

Dear God, we thank you for the gift of your Son, Jesus Christ. We are grateful for his sacrifice on the cross, which offers us forgiveness, hope, and salvation. May we never forget the depth of your love and the power of the cross to transform our lives. Amen.

Living with Faith:

- This week, spend some time reflecting on the significance of the cross in your faith journey. How does it impact your understanding of God's love and grace?

- Consider wearing a cross or other symbol of your faith as a reminder of Christ's sacrifice.

- Share the message of the cross with someone who might be struggling or searching for meaning in their life. Offer them words of encouragement and hope.

Notes:_____
_____
_____

Sunday, September 21

- Twenty-fifth Sunday in Ordinary Time

First Reading: Amos 8: 4-7

Responsorial Psalm: Psalms 113: 1-2, 4-6, 7-8

Second Reading: First Timothy 2: 1-8

Alleluia: Second Corinthians 8: 9

Gospel: Luke 16: 1-13

Lectionary: 135

This Sunday's readings delve into themes of justice, stewardship, and the importance of using our resources wisely. We'll encounter a call for social justice, practical advice for prayer, and a parable that challenges our understanding of wealth.

A Cry for Justice (Amos 8: 4-7):

4 Hear this, you that crush the poor, and make the needy of the land to fail,

5 Saying: When will the month be over, and we shall sell our wares: and the sabbath, and we shall open the corn: that we may lessen the measure, and increase the sicle, and may convey in deceitful balances,

6 That we may possess the needy for money, and the poor for a pair of shoes, and may sell the refuse of the corn?

7 The Lord hath sworn against the pride of Jacob: surely I will never forget all their works.

The Book of Amos opens the service with a strong message. The prophet condemns the exploitation of the poor and the manipulation of the justice system for personal gain. This passage reminds us of God's concern for the marginalized and the importance of fairness in society.

Responsorial Psalm: Psalms
113: 1-2, 4-6, 7-8

R. (1a, 7b) Praise the Lord who lifts up the poor.

or

R. Alleluia.

1 Praise the Lord, ye children: praise ye the name of the Lord.

2 Blessed be the name of the Lord, from henceforth now and for ever.

R. Praise the Lord who lifts up the poor.

or

R. Alleluia.

4 The Lord is high above all nations; and his glory above the heavens.

5 Who is as the Lord our God, who dwelleth on high:

6 And looketh down on the low things in heaven and in earth?

R. Praise the Lord who lifts up the poor.

or

R. Alleluia.

7 Raising up the needy from the earth, and lifting up the poor out of the dunghill:

8 That he may place him with princes, with the princes of his people.

R. Praise the Lord who lifts up the poor.

or

R. Alleluia.

Praying for All (First Timothy 2: 1-8):

1 I desire therefore, first of all, that supplications, prayers, intercessions, and thanksgivings be made for all men:

2 For kings, and for all that are in high station: that we may lead a quiet and a peaceable life in all piety and chastity.

3 For this is good and acceptable in the sight of God our Saviour,

4 Who will have all men to be saved, and to come to the knowledge of the truth.

5 For there is one God, and one mediator of God and men, the man Christ Jesus:

6 Who gave himself a redemption for all, a testimony in due times.

7 Whereunto I am appointed a preacher and an apostle, (I say the truth, I lie not,) a doctor of the Gentiles in faith and truth.

8 I will therefore that men pray in every place, lifting up pure hands, without anger and contention.

The First Letter to Timothy offers practical advice for prayer. The passage encourages us to pray for all people, including those in authority, so that we can live peaceful and quiet lives. This call to pray for everyone, regardless of background or belief, reflects God's universal love.

Alleluia: Second Corinthians 8: 9

R. Alleluia, alleluia.

9 Though our Lord Jesus Christ was rich, he became poor, so that by his poverty you might become rich.

R. Alleluia, alleluia.

The Parable of the Dishonest Manager (Luke 16: 1-13):

1 And he said also to his disciples: There was a certain rich man who had a steward: and the same was accused unto him, that he had wasted his goods.

2 And he called him, and said to him: How is it that I hear this of thee? give an account of thy stewardship: for now thou canst be steward no longer.

3 And the steward said within himself: What shall I do, because my lord taketh away from me the stewardship? To dig I am not able; to beg I am ashamed.

4 I know what I will do, that when I shall be removed from the stewardship, they may receive me into their houses.

5 Therefore calling together every one of his lord's debtors, he said to the first: How much dost thou owe my lord?

6 But he said: An hundred barrels of oil. And he said to him: Take thy bill and sit down quickly, and write fifty.

7 Then he said to another: And how much dost thou owe? Who said: An hundred quarters of wheat. He said to him: Take thy bill, and write eighty.

8 And the lord commended the unjust steward, forasmuch as he had done wisely: for the children of this world are wiser in their generation than the children of light.

9 And I say to you: Make unto you friends of the mammon of iniquity; that when you shall fail, they may receive you into everlasting dwellings.

10 He that is faithful in that which is least, is faithful also in that which is greater: and he that is unjust in that which is little, is unjust also in that which is greater.

11 If then you have not been faithful in the unjust mammon; who will trust you with that which is the true?

12 And if you have not been faithful in that which is another's; who will give you that which is your own?

13 No servant can serve two masters: for either he will hate the one, and love the other; or he will hold to the one, and despise the other. You cannot serve God and mammon.

The Gospel of Luke presents a parable that, at first glance, seems counterintuitive. Jesus tells the story of a dishonest manager who is praised for his shrewdness (though not his dishonesty) in securing his future. The key takeaway is not to condone dishonesty, but to emphasize the importance of being wise stewards of the resources entrusted to us.

Reflect and Respond:

- How can you advocate for justice and fairness in your community?

- The reading from Timothy encourages us to pray for all people. Consider creating a prayer list that includes those in authority, those in need, and people of different backgrounds.

- The parable challenges our understanding of wealth. What does true wealth mean to you? How can you be a wiser steward of the resources you have been given?

A Prayer for Justice and Stewardship:

Dear God, grant us the courage to speak out against injustice and the wisdom to use our resources wisely. Help us to pray for all people, reflecting your universal love. May we be faithful stewards of all that you have entrusted to us. Amen.

Living with Purpose:

- This week, research an organization working towards social justice in your community. Consider volunteering your time or donating to their cause.

- Spend some time reflecting on your own spending habits.

Are there ways you can be more mindful and use your resources to support causes you care about?

- Talk to someone you trust about your understanding of wealth and purpose. Sharing perspectives can lead to deeper insights and a more fulfilling life.

Notes:_____

_____

_____

_____

_____

_____

_____

_____

_____

_____

_____

_____

_____

_____

_____

_____

_____

_____

Sunday, September 28

- Twenty-sixth Sunday in Ordinary Time

First Reading: Amos 6: 1a, 4-7

Responsorial Psalm: Psalms 146: 7, 8-9, 9-10

Second Reading: First Timothy 6: 11-16

Alleluia: Second Corinthians 8: 9

Gospel: Luke 16: 19-31

Lectionary: 138

This Sunday's readings delve into themes of living a simple life, the dangers of materialism, and the contrasting fates of those who prioritize worldly possessions versus those who prioritize God.

Beware the Perils of Wealth (Amos 6: 1a, 4-7):

1a Thus says the LORD the God of hosts: Woe to you that are wealthy in Sion!

4 You that sleep upon beds of ivory, and are wanton on your couches: that eat the lambs out of the flock, and the calves out of the midst of the herd;

5 You that sing to the sound of the psaltery: they have thought themselves to have instruments of music like David;

6 That drink wine in bowls, and anoint themselves with the best ointments: and they are not concerned for the affliction of Joseph.

7 Wherefore now they shall go captive at the head of them that go into captivity: and the faction of the luxurious ones shall be taken away.

The Book of Amos opens the service with a stern warning. The prophet condemns the wealthy Israelites who live in extravagant luxury while ignoring the suffering of the poor. This passage reminds us of the dangers of materialism and the importance of using our resources for good.

Responsorial Psalm: Psalms 146: 7, 8-9, 9-10

R. (1b) Praise the Lord, my soul!

Or R. Alleluia.

7 Who keepeth truth for ever: who executeth judgment for them that suffer wrong: who giveth food to the hungry. The Lord looseth them that are fettered:

R. Praise the Lord, my soul!

Or R. Alleluia.

8 The Lord enlighteneth the blind. The Lord lifteth up them that are cast down: the Lord loveth the just.

9a The Lord keepeth the strangers.

R. Praise the Lord, my soul!

Or R. Alleluia.

9bc He will support the fatherless and the widow: and the ways of sinners he will destroy.

10 The Lord shall reign for ever: thy God, O Sion, unto generation and generation.

R. Praise the Lord, my soul!

Or R. Alleluia.

Fight the Good Fight (First Timothy 6: 11-16):

11 But thou, O man of God, fly these things: and pursue justice, godliness, faith, charity, patience, mildness.

12 Fight the good fight of faith: lay hold on eternal life, whereunto thou art called, and hast confessed a good confession before many witnesses.

13 I charge thee before God, who quickeneth all things, and before Christ Jesus, who gave testimony under Pontius Pilate, a good confession,

14 That thou keep the commandment without spot, blameless, unto the coming of our Lord Jesus Christ,

15 Which in his times he shall shew who is the Blessed and only Mighty, the King of kings, and Lord of lords;

16 Who only hath immortality, and inhabiteth light inaccessible, whom no man hath seen, nor can see: to whom be honour and empire everlasting. Amen.

The First Letter to Timothy offers guidance for living a faithful life. The passage urges us to fight the good fight of faith and pursue righteousness, contentment, and love. It warns against the destructive pursuit of wealth and emphasizes the importance of trusting in God, who provides all that we need.

Alleluia: Second Corinthians 8: 9

R. Alleluia, alleluia.

9 Though our Lord Jesus Christ was rich, he became poor, so that by his poverty you might become rich.

R. Alleluia, alleluia.

The Rich Man and Lazarus (Luke 16: 19-31):

19 There was a certain rich man, who was clothed in purple and fine linen; and feasted sumptuously every day.

20 And there was a certain beggar, named Lazarus, who lay at his gate, full of sores,

21 Desiring to be filled with the crumbs that fell from the rich man's table, and no one did give him; moreover the dogs came, and licked his sores.

22 And it came to pass, that the beggar died, and was carried by the angels into Abraham's bosom. And the rich man also died: and he was buried in hell.

23 And lifting up his eyes when he was in torments, he saw Abraham afar off, and Lazarus in his bosom:

24 And he cried, and said: Father Abraham, have mercy on me, and send Lazarus, that he may dip the tip of his finger in water, to cool my tongue: for I am tormented in this flame.

25 And Abraham said to him: Son, remember that thou didst receive good things in thy lifetime, and likewise Lazareth evil things, but now he is comforted; and thou art tormented.

26 And besides all this, between us and you, there is fixed a great chaos: so that they who would pass from hence to you, cannot, nor from thence come hither.

27 And he said: Then, father, I beseech thee, that thou wouldst send him to my father's house, for I have five brethren,

28 That he may testify unto them, lest they also come into this place of torments.

29 And Abraham said to him: They have Moses and the prophets; let them hear them.

30 But he said: No, father Abraham: but if one went to them from the dead, they will do penance.

31 And he said to him: If they hear not Moses and the prophets, neither will they believe, if one rise again from the dead.

The Gospel of Luke presents the parable of the rich man and Lazarus. The rich man lives a life of luxury, while Lazarus, a poor beggar, lies at his gate. When both die, their fates are reversed. The rich man finds himself in torment, while Lazarus finds comfort in Abraham's bosom. This parable serves as a stark reminder that true wealth is not found in material possessions, but in a relationship with God.

Reflect and Respond:

- How can you cultivate a more simple and content lifestyle?

- The reading from Timothy talks about fighting the good fight of faith. What challenges do you face in living your faith?

- The parable challenges us to examine our priorities. Where does your true treasure lie – in material possessions or in your relationship with God?

A Prayer for Contentment:

Dear God, help us to avoid the allure of material possessions and to find contentment in your presence. Grant us the strength to fight the good fight of faith and to prioritize our relationship with you above all else. May we use our resources wisely to help those in need. Amen.

Living with Less:

- This week, challenge yourself to a "detox" from materialism. Spend less time shopping or browsing online. Consider donating some of your unused belongings to charity.

- Reflect on your talents and resources. How can you use them to serve others and make a positive impact in your community?

- Talk to someone you trust about your faith journey and the challenges you face. Sharing your struggles can be a source of strength and encouragement.

Notes:_____

October2025

Sunday, October 5

- **Twenty-seventh Sunday in Ordinary Time**

First Reading: Habakkuk 1: 2-3; 2: 2-4

Responsorial Psalm: Psalms 95: 1-2, 6-7, 8-9

Second Reading: Second Timothy 1: 6-8, 13-14

Alleluia: First Peter 1: 25

Gospel: Luke 17: 5-10

Lectionary: 141

This Sunday's readings center around the themes of faith, perseverance, and the importance of humility in our spiritual journeys. We'll encounter a prophet lamenting injustice, a call to fan the flame of faith, and a reminder that true service comes from a place of humility.

Waiting for Justice (Habakkuk 1: 2-3; 2: 2-4):

2 How long, O Lord, shall I cry, and thou wilt not hear? shall I cry out to thee suffering violence, and thou wilt not save?

3 Why hast thou shewn me iniquity and grievance, to see rapine and injustice before me? and there is a judgment, but opposition is more powerful.

2:2 And the Lord answered me, and said: Write the vision, and make it plain upon tables: that he that readeth it may run over it.

3 For as yet the vision is far off, and it shall appear at the end, and shall not lie: if it make any delay, wait for it: for it shall surely come, and it shall not be slack.

4 Behold, he that is unbelieving, his soul shall not be right in himself: but the just shall live in his faith.

The Book of Habakkuk opens the service with a prophet's cry of frustration. Habakkuk witnesses injustice and wonders why God seems silent. The passage, while acknowledging challenges, also offers a message of hope. God will act in His time, and the righteous will live by faith.

R. (8) If today you hear his voice, harden not your hearts.

1 Come let us praise the Lord with joy: let us joyfully sing to God our saviour.

2 Let us come before his presence with thanksgiving; and make a joyful noise to him with psalms.

R. If today you hear his voice, harden not your hearts.

6 Come let us adore and fall down: and weep before the Lord that made us.

7 For he is the Lord our God: and we are the people of his pasture and the sheep of his hand.

R. If today you hear his voice, harden not your hearts.

8 Today if you shall hear his voice, harden not your hearts:

9 As in the provocation, according to the day of temptation in the wilderness: where your fathers tempted me, they proved me, and saw my works.

R. If today you hear his voice, harden not your hearts.

Fanning the Flame of Faith (Second Timothy 1: 6-8, 13-14):

6 For which cause I admonish thee, that thou stir up the grace of God which is in thee, by the imposition of my hands.

7 For God hath not given us the spirit of fear: but of power, and of love, and of sobriety.

8 Be not thou therefore ashamed of the testimony of our Lord, nor of me his prisoner: but labour with the gospel, according to the power of God,

13 Hold the form of sound words, which thou hast heard of me in faith, and in the love which is in Christ Jesus.

14 Keep the good thing committed to thy trust by the Holy Ghost, who dwelleth in us.

The Second Letter to Timothy offers encouragement for perseverance in the faith. Paul reminds Timothy, and by extension all believers, to fan into flame the gift of faith that is within us. The passage emphasizes the importance of holding fast to the teachings we have received and living a life of courage and love.

Alleluia: First Peter 1: 25

R. Alleluia, alleluia.

25 The word of the Lord remains forever. This is the word that has been proclaimed to you.

R. Alleluia, alleluia.

Faithful Servants (Luke 17: 5-10):

5 And the apostles said to the Lord: Increase our faith.

6 And the Lord said: If you had faith like to a grain of mustard seed, you might say to this mulberry tree, Be thou rooted up, and be thou transplanted into the sea: and it would obey you.

7 But which of you having a servant ploughing, or feeding cattle, will say to him, when he is come from the field: Immediately go, sit down to meat:

8 And will not rather say to him: Make ready my supper, and gird thyself, and serve me, whilst I eat and drink, and afterwards thou shalt eat and drink?

9 Doth he thank that servant, for doing the things which he commanded him?

10 I think not. So you also, when you shall have done all these things that are commanded you, say: We are unprofitable servants; we have done that which we ought to do.

The Gospel of Luke presents a familiar passage about faith. The disciples ask Jesus to increase their faith, and He replies with a surprising analogy. Even a small amount of faith, like a mustard seed, can accomplish great things. The key takeaway is not about the quantity of faith, but about using it to serve God faithfully. Jesus reminds us that as servants, we are simply doing what we are obligated to do.

Reflect and Respond:

- How can you cultivate a stronger sense of faith in your daily life?

- The reading from Timothy talks about fanning the flame of faith. What practices help you keep your faith alive?

- The parable reminds us that we are servants. How can you approach your daily tasks with an attitude of service to God?

A Prayer for Growth:

Dear God, help us to grow in faith, trusting in your timing even when we don't understand. Grant us the courage to

persevere in our faith journeys and to fan the flame of faith within us. May we serve you with humility and faithfulness, recognizing that all we have and all we do comes from you. Amen.

Living with Faith:

- This week, set aside some time for daily prayer or meditation. Even a few minutes can make a difference in strengthening your connection with God.

- Consider memorizing a scripture passage or a prayer that resonates with you. Having these words readily available can be a source of comfort and strength.

- Look for opportunities to serve others throughout the week. Simple acts of kindness can be a powerful way to live out your faith.

Notes:_____

Sunday, October 12

- Twenty-eighth Sunday in Ordinary Time

First Reading: Second Kings 5: 14-17

Responsorial Psalm: Psalms 98: 1, 2-3ab, 3c-4

Second Reading: Second Timothy 2: 8-13

Alleluia: First Thessalonians 5: 18

Gospel: Luke 17: 11-19

Lectionary: 144

This Sunday's readings explore themes of healing, faithfulness, and expressing gratitude for God's blessings. We'll encounter a story of miraculous healing, a call to persevere in following Christ, and a reminder to thank God for his goodness.

Naaman Seeks Healing (Second Kings 5: 14-17):

14 Then he went down, and washed in the Jordan seven times: according to the word of the man of God, and his flesh was restored, like the flesh of a little child, and he was made clean.

15 And returning to the man of God with all his train, be came, and stood before him, and said: In truth, I know there is no other God in all the earth, but only in Israel: I beseech thee therefore take a blessing of thy servant.

16 But he answered: As the Lord liveth, before whom I stand, I will receive none. And when he pressed him, he still refused.

17 And Naaman said: As thou wilt: but I beseech thee, grant to me thy servant, to take from hence two mules' burden of earth: for thy servant will not henceforth offer holocaust, or victim, to other gods, but to the Lord.

The Book of Kings opens the service with a story of faith and obedience. Naaman, a Syrian commander with leprosy, seeks healing from the prophet Elisha. He follows the prophet's instructions and is miraculously cured. This passage highlights the power of God to heal and the importance of faith in receiving his blessings.

Responsorial Psalm: Psalms 98: 1, 2-3ab, 3c-4

R. (2b) The Lord has revealed to the nations his saving power.

1 Sing ye to the Lord anew canticle: because he hath done wonderful things. His right hand hath wrought for him salvation, and his arm is holy.

R. The Lord has revealed to the nations his saving power.

2 The Lord hath made known his salvation: he hath revealed his justice in the sight of the Gentiles.

3ab He hath remembered his mercy his truth toward the house of Israel.

R. The Lord has revealed to the nations his saving power.

3c All the ends of the earth have seen the salvation of our God.

4 Sing joyfully to God, all the earth; make melody, rejoice and sing.

R. The Lord has revealed to the nations his saving power.

Perseverance in Faith (Second Timothy 2: 8-13):

8 Be mindful that the Lord Jesus Christ is risen again from the dead, of the seed of David, according to my gospel.

9 Wherein I labour even unto bands, as an evildoer; but the word of God is not bound.

10 Therefore I endure all things for the sake of the elect, that they also may obtain the salvation, which is in Christ Jesus, with heavenly glory.

11 A faithful saying: for if we be dead with him, we shall live also with him.

12 If we suffer, we shall also reign with him. If we deny him, he will also deny us.

13 If we believe not, he continueth faithful, he can not deny himself.

The Second Letter to Timothy offers encouragement for those facing challenges in their faith journey. Paul uses the metaphor of a soldier to emphasize the importance of perseverance and discipline. Following Christ requires commitment and dedication, but the reward is eternal life.

Alleluia: First Thessalonians 5: 18

R. Alleluia, alleluia.

18 In all circumstances, give thanks, for this is the will of God for you in Christ Jesus.

R. Alleluia, alleluia.

Gratitude for Healing (Luke 17: 11-19):

11 And it came to pass, as he was going to Jerusalem, he passed through the midst of Samaria and Galilee.

12 And as he entered into a certain town, there met him ten men that were lepers, who stood afar off:

13 And lifted up their voice, saying: Jesus, master, have mercy on us.

14 Whom when he saw, he said: Go, shew yourselves to the priests. And it came to pass, as they went, they were made clean.

15 And one of them, when he saw that he was made clean, went back, with a loud voice glorifying God.

16 And he fell on his face before his feet, giving thanks: and this was a Samaritan.

17 And Jesus answering, said, Were not ten made clean? and where are the nine?

18 There is no one found to return and give glory to God, but this stranger.

19 And he said to him: Arise, go thy way; for thy faith hath made thee whole.

The Gospel of Luke presents the story of Jesus healing ten lepers. While all ten are cleansed, only one returns to thank Jesus. This parable reminds us of the importance of expressing gratitude for God's blessings, both big and small.

Reflect and Respond:

- Can you recall a time in your life when you experienced healing, whether physical, emotional, or spiritual?

- The reading from Timothy talks about perseverance. What challenges do you face in your faith journey, and how can you persevere?

- The parable reminds us to be grateful. Take some time this week to reflect on the blessings in your life and express your gratitude to God.

A Prayer for Gratitude:

Dear God, we thank you for your healing power and your abundant blessings. Grant us the faith to persevere in our commitment to you. May we never take your goodness for granted, but always offer our thanks with grateful hearts. Amen.

Living with Gratitude:

- This week, keep a gratitude journal. Each day, write down three things you are grateful for, big or small. Reflecting on these blessings can shift your perspective and cultivate a more grateful heart.

- Consider reaching out to someone who has been a source of support or encouragement in your life. Express your gratitude for their presence in your life.

- Pay attention to the beauty and wonder of the world around you. Seeing the world through a lens of gratitude can deepen your appreciation for God's creation.

Notes:_____
_____

Sunday, October 19

- Twenty-ninth Sunday in Ordinary Time

First Reading: Exodus 17: 8-13

Responsorial Psalm: Psalms 121: 1-2, 3-4, 5-6, 7-8

Second Reading: Second Timothy 3: 14 - 4: 2

Alleluia: Hebrews 4: 12

Gospel: Luke 18: 1-8

Lectionary: 147

This Sunday's readings delve into themes of perseverance, the importance of scripture, and the power of persistent prayer. We'll encounter a story of the Israelites battling the Amalekites, a call to remain faithful to scripture, and the parable of the persistent widow.

Victory Through Perseverance (Exodus 17: 8-13):

8 And Amalec came, and fought against Israel in Raphidim.

9 And Moses said to Josue: Choose out men: and go out and fight against Amalec: tomorrow I will stand on the top of the hill having the rod of God in my hand.

10 Josue did as Moses had spoken, and he fought against Amalec; but Moses, and Aaron, and Hur went up upon the top of the hill.

11 And when Moses lifted up his hands, Israel overcame: but if he let them down a little, Amalec overcame.

12 And Moses' hands were heavy: so they took a stone, and put under him, and he sat on it: and Aaron and Hur stayed up his hands on both sides. And it came to pass that his hands were not weary until sunset.

13 And Josue put Amalec and his people to flight, by the edge of the sword.

The Book of Exodus opens the service with a story that

highlights the importance of perseverance. The Israelites are locked in battle with the Amalekites, and their success hinges on Moses holding his staff aloft. This passage reminds us that with faith and determination, we can overcome challenges.

Responsorial Psalm: Psalms 121: 1-2, 3-4, 5-6, 7-8

R. (2) Our help is from the Lord, who made heaven and earth.

1 I have lifted up my eyes to the mountains, from whence help shall come to me.

2 My help is from the Lord, who made heaven and earth.

R. Our help is from the Lord, who made heaven and earth.

3 May he not suffer thy foot to be moved: neither let him slumber that keepeth thee.

4 Behold he shall neither slumber nor sleep, that keepeth Israel.

R. Our help is from the Lord, who made heaven and earth.

5 The Lord is thy keeper, the Lord is thy protection upon thy right hand.

6 The sun shall not burn thee by day: nor the moon by night.

R. Our help is from the Lord, who made heaven and earth.

7 The Lord keepeth thee from all evil: may the Lord keep thy soul.

8 May the Lord keep thy going in and thy going out; from henceforth now and for ever.

R. Our help is from the Lord, who made heaven and earth.

Rooted in Scripture (Second Timothy 3: 14 – 4: 2):

14 But continue thou in those things which thou hast learned, and which have been committed to thee: knowing of whom thou hast learned them;

15 And because from thy infancy thou hast known the holy scriptures, which can instruct thee to salvation, by the faith which is in Christ Jesus.

16 All scripture, inspired of God, is profitable to teach, to reprove, to correct, to instruct in justice,

17 That the man of God may be perfect, furnished to every good work.

4:1 I charge thee, before God and Jesus Christ, who shall judge the living and the dead, by his coming, and his kingdom:

2 Preach the word: be instant in season, out of season: reprove, entreat, rebuke in all patience and doctrine.

The Second Letter to Timothy emphasizes the importance of scripture in our faith journey. Paul reminds Timothy, and by extension all believers, that scripture is God-breathed and equips us for every good work. The passage encourages us to faithfully proclaim the message of the gospel.

Alleluia: Hebrews 4: 12

R. Alleluia, alleluia.

12 The word of God is living and effective, discerning reflections and thoughts of the heart.

R. Alleluia, alleluia.

The Persistent Widow (Luke 18: 1-8):

1 And he spoke also a parable to them, that we ought always to pray, and not to faint,

2 Saying: There was a judge in a certain city, who feared not God, nor regarded man.

3 And there was a certain widow in that city, and she came to him, saying: Avenge me of my adversary.

4 And he would not for a long time. But afterwards he said within himself: Although I fear not God, nor regard man,

5 Yet because this widow is troublesome to me, I will avenge her, lest continually coming she weary me.

6 And the Lord said: Hear what the unjust judge saith.

7 And will not God revenge his elect who cry to him day and night: and will he have patience in their regard?

8 I say to you, that he will quickly revenge them. But yet the Son of man, when he cometh, shall he find, think you, faith on earth?

The Gospel of Luke presents the parable of the persistent widow. A poor widow relentlessly seeks justice from a corrupt judge. Though he initially ignores her, her persistence eventually wears him down. Jesus uses this parable to teach about the importance of persistent prayer. Just as the widow would not give up, we should not give up in seeking God's help.

Reflect and Respond:

- Can you think of a time in your life when perseverance helped you overcome a challenge?

- The reading from Timothy emphasizes scripture. How can you make studying scripture a more regular part of your life?

- The parable reminds us of the power of persistent prayer. Is there something you have been praying for? Don't give up – keep bringing your requests to God with faith.

A Prayer for Perseverance:

Dear God, grant us the strength to persevere in the face of challenges. Help us to remain rooted in your word and to find guidance and encouragement from scripture. May we learn from the example of the persistent widow and bring our prayers to you with unwavering faith. Amen.

Living with Faith:

- This week, choose a challenging task or goal you've been putting off. Start small and take consistent steps towards achieving it. Remember, perseverance is key.

- Dedicate some time each day to reading scripture. Even a few verses can make a difference. Consider joining a Bible study group for deeper reflection and discussion.

- Write down your prayer requests and keep them somewhere you can see them daily. This will help you stay focused and remind you to keep praying, even if you don't see an immediate answer.

Notes:_____

_____
_____
_____
_____
_____
_____
_____
_____
_____

_____
_____
_____
_____
_____
_____
_____
_____
_____
_____
_____
_____
_____
_____
_____
_____
_____
_____
_____
_____
_____
_____
_____
_____
_____
_____
_____
_____
_____

Sunday, October 26

- Thirtieth Sunday in Ordinary Time

First Reading: Sirach 35: 12-14, 16-18

Responsorial Psalm: Psalms 34: 2-3, 17-18, 19, 23

Second Reading: Second Timothy 4: 6-8, 16-18

Alleluia: Second Corinthians 5: 19

Gospel: Luke 18: 9-14

Lectionary: 150

This Sunday, the final one in Ordinary Time before the liturgical season changes, prompts us to reflect on humility, self-examination, and the importance of a prayer life rooted in truth.

The Cry of the Oppressed (Sirach 35: 12-14, 16-18):

12 And look not upon an unjust sacrifice, for the Lord is judge, and there is not with him respect of person.

13 The Lord will not accept any person against a poor man, and he will hear the prayer of him that is wronged.

14 He will not despise the prayers of the fatherless; nor the widow, when she poureth out her complaint.

16 For from the cheek they go up even to heaven, and the Lord that heareth will not be delighted with them.

17 He that adoreth God with joy, shall be accepted, and his prayer shall approach even to the clouds.

18 The prayer of him that humbleth himself, shall pierce the clouds: and till it come nigh he will not be comforted: and he will not depart till the most High behold.

The Book of Sirach opens the service with a powerful message about justice. The passage reminds us that God hears the cry of the oppressed and will hold the wicked accountable.

It's a call to live with integrity and to stand up for those who are unable to stand up for themselves.

R. (7a) The Lord hears the cry of the poor.

2 I will bless the Lord at all times, his praise shall be always in my mouth.

3 In the Lord shall my soul be praised: let the meek hear and rejoice.

R. The Lord hears the cry of the poor.

17 But the countenance of the Lord is against them that do evil things: to cut off the remembrance of them from the earth.

18 The just cried, and the Lord heard them: and delivered them out of all their troubles.

R. The Lord hears the cry of the poor.

19 The Lord is nigh unto them that are of a contrite heart: and he will save the humble of spirit.

23 The Lord will redeem the souls of his servants: and none of them that trust in him shall offend.

R. The Lord hears the cry of the poor.

Finishing the Race (Second Timothy 4: 6-8, 16-18):

---

6 For I am even now ready to be sacrificed: and the time of my dissolution is at hand.

7 I have fought a good fight, I have finished my course, I have kept the faith.

8 As to the rest, there is laid up for me a crown of justice, which the Lord the just judge will render to me in that day: and not only to me, but to them also that love his coming. Make haste to come to me quickly.

16 At my first answer no man stood with me, but all forsook me: may it not be laid to their charge.

17 But the Lord stood by me, and strengthened me, that by me the preaching may be accomplished, and that all the Gentiles may hear: and I

was delivered out of the mouth of the lion.

18 The Lord hath delivered me from every evil work: and will preserve me unto his heavenly kingdom, to whom be glory for ever and ever. Amen.

The Second Letter to Timothy offers a message of encouragement from Paul near the end of his life. He uses the metaphor of a race to describe the Christian life. Paul emphasizes the importance of finishing the race, having fought the good fight and kept the faith. The passage offers a sense of hope and perseverance for those who remain faithful.

Alleluia: Second Corinthians 5: 19

R. Alleluia, alleluia.

19 God was reconciling the world to himself in Christ, and entrusting to us the message of salvation.

R. Alleluia, alleluia.

The Pharisee and the Tax Collector (Luke 18: 9-14):

9 And to some who trusted in themselves as just, and despised others, he spoke also this parable:

10 Two men went up into the temple to pray: the one a Pharisee, and the other a publican.

11 The Pharisee standing, prayed thus with himself: O God, I give thee thanks that I am not as the rest of men, extortioners, unjust, adulterers, as also is this publican.

12 I fast twice in a week: I give tithes of all that I possess.

13 And the publican, standing afar off, would not so much as lift up his eyes towards heaven; but struck his breast, saying: O God, be merciful to me a sinner.

14 I say to you, this man went down into his house justified rather than the other: because every one that exalteth himself, shall be humbled: and he that humbleth himself, shall be exalted.

The Gospel of Luke presents the parable of the Pharisee and the tax collector. The Pharisee boasts of his good deeds, while the tax collector humbly begs for God's mercy. Jesus reminds us that true prayer comes from a heart of humility, acknowledging our shortcomings and seeking God's forgiveness.

shortcomings and seek your forgiveness with sincere hearts. May our prayers be rooted in truth and gratitude, reflecting our dependence on you. Amen.

Reflect and Respond:

- How can you advocate for justice and fairness in your community?

- The reading from Timothy talks about finishing the race. Consider your own faith journey. What challenges do you face, and how can you persevere?

- The parable challenges us to examine our hearts. When you pray, do you approach God with an attitude of humility or self-righteousness?

A Prayer for Humility:

Dear God, grant us the humility to see ourselves as you see us. Help us to acknowledge our

Living with Humility:

- This week, take some time for introspection. Consider your strengths and weaknesses. How can you cultivate a more humble attitude in your interactions with others?

- Look for opportunities to serve others without expecting anything in return. True service comes from a place of humility.

- Spend some time in prayer each day. Focus on expressing gratitude for God's blessings and acknowledging your need for his grace.

Notes:_____
_____

November 2025

Sunday, November 2

- **Commemoration of All the Faithful Departed (All Souls) - Solemnity**

First Reading: Wisdom 3: 1-9

Responsorial Psalm: Psalms 23: 1-3a, 3b-4, 5, 6

Second Reading: Romans 6: 3-9

Alleluia: Matthew 25: 34

Gospel: John 6: 37-40

Lectionary: 668

All Souls' Day, a solemn observance in the Catholic Church, falls on November 2nd. Today, we remember and pray for those who have died, particularly those who may still be undergoing purification before entering Heaven.

This Sunday's readings offer comfort, hope, and a reminder of the enduring power of God's love.

The Righteous Have No Fear (Wisdom 3: 1-9):

1 But the souls of the just are in the hand of God, and the torment of death shall not touch them.

2 In the sight of the unwise they seemed to die: and their departure was taken for misery:

3 And their going away from us, for utter destruction: but they are in peace.

4 And though in the sight of men they suffered torments, their hope is full of immortality.

5 Afflicted in few things, in many they shall be well rewarded: because God hath tried them, and found them worthy of himself.

6 As gold in the furnace he hath proved them, and as a victim of a holocaust he hath received them, and in time there shall be respect had to them.

7 The just shall shine, and shall run to and fro like sparks among the reeds.

8 They shall judge nations, and rule over people, and their Lord shall reign for ever.

9 They that trust in him, shall understand the truth: and they that are faithful in love shall rest in him: for grace and peace is to his elect.

The Book of Wisdom opens the service with a message of comfort for those who mourn. The passage assures us that the souls of the righteous are safe in God's hands, even though they may appear to be dead. This reading offers hope for the afterlife and the ultimate victory of good over evil.

Responsorial Psalm: Psalms 23: 1-3a, 3b-4, 5, 6

R. (1) The Lord is my shepherd; there is nothing I shall want.

or

R. Though I walk in the valley of darkness, I fear no evil, for you are with me.

1 The Lord ruleth me: and I shall want nothing.

2 He hath set me in a place of pasture. He hath brought me up, on the water of refreshment:

3a He hath converted my soul.

R. The Lord is my shepherd; there is nothing I shall want.

or

R. Though I walk in the valley of darkness, I fear no evil, for you are with me.

3b He hath led me on the paths of justice, for his own name's sake.

4 For though I should walk in the midst of the shadow of death, I will fear no evils, for thou art with me. Thy rod and thy staff, they have comforted me.

R. The Lord is my shepherd; there is nothing I shall want.

or

R. Though I walk in the valley of darkness, I fear no evil, for you are with me.

5 Thou hast prepared a table before me against them that afflict me. Thou hast anointed my head with oil; and my chalice which inebriateth me, how goodly is it!

R. The Lord is my shepherd; there is nothing I shall want.

or

R. Though I walk in the valley of darkness, I fear no evil, for you are with me.

6 And thy mercy will follow me all the days of my life. And that I may dwell in the house of the Lord unto length of days.

R. The Lord is my shepherd; there is nothing I shall want.

or

R. Though I walk in the valley of darkness, I fear no evil, for you are with me.

United in Christ (Romans 5: 5-11 orRomans 6: 3-9):

5 And hope confoundeth not: because the charity of God is poured forth in our hearts, by the Holy Ghost, who is given to us.

6 For why did Christ, when as yet we were weak, according to the time, die for the ungodly?

7 For scarce for a just man will one die; yet perhaps for a good man some one would dare to die.

8 But God commendeth his charity towards us; because when as yet we were sinners, according to the time,

9 Christ died for us; much more therefore, being now justified by his blood, shall we be saved from wrath through him.

10 For if, when we were enemies, we were reconciled to God by the death of his Son; much more, being reconciled, shall we be saved by his life.

11 And not only so; but also we glory in God, through our Lord Jesus Christ, by whom we have now received reconciliation.

Or

3 Know you not that all we, who are baptized in Christ Jesus, are baptized in his death?

4 For we are buried together with him by baptism into death; that as Christ is risen from the dead by the glory of the Father, so we also may walk in newness of life.

5 For if we have been planted together in the likeness of his death, we shall be also in the likeness of his resurrection.

6 Knowing this, that our old man is crucified with him, that the body of sin may be destroyed, to the end that we may serve sin no longer.

7 For he that is dead is justified from sin.

8 Now if we be dead with Christ, we believe that we shall live also together with Christ:

9 Knowing that Christ rising again from the dead, dieth now no more, death shall no more have dominion over him.

The Letter to the Romans speaks of the transformative power of baptism. Through baptism, we die to sin and are raised to new life in Christ. The passage assures us that if we are united with Christ in his death, we will also be united with him in his resurrection. This offers hope for the eternal life that awaits believers.

Alleluia: Matthew 25: 34

R. Alleluia, alleluia.

34 Come, you who are blessed by my Father; inherit the Kingdom prepared for you from the foundation of the world.

R. Alleluia, alleluia.

All Who Come to Me (John 6: 37-40):

37 All that the Father giveth to me shall come to me; and him that cometh to me, I will not cast out.

38 Because I came down from heaven, not to do my own will, but the will of him that sent me.

39 Now this is the will of the Father who sent me: that of all that he hath given me, I should lose nothing; but should raise it up again in the last day.

40 And this is the will of my Father that sent me: that every one who seeth the Son, and believeth in him,

may have life everlasting, and I will raise him up in the last day.

The Gospel of John presents a powerful promise from Jesus. He declares that whoever comes to him will not be cast out, and that he will raise them up on the last day. This passage emphasizes God's universal love and his desire for all people to be saved.

Reflect and Respond:

- Take some time today to remember loved ones who have passed away. Share stories or memories of them with others.

- The readings offer comfort and hope. Is there someone in your life who is grieving? Offer them words of encouragement and support.

- Consider praying a rosary or attending a special Mass dedicated to the faithful departed.

A Prayer for the Faithful Departed:

Dear God, we remember today all those who have passed away, especially [name specific individuals you wish to remember]. Grant them eternal rest and peace. May your light shine upon them, and may they be cleansed of all sin. We pray that they may enjoy the fullness of your love in the company of your saints. Amen.

Living with Hope:

- All Souls' Day is a time to reflect on our own mortality. Consider making a will or planning your funeral arrangements to give your loved ones peace of mind.

- Look for ways to honor the memory of those who have passed away. Donate to a charity they supported, plant a tree in their memory, or simply share stories about them with future generations.

- All Souls' Day is a reminder that death is not the end. Cling to the hope of eternal life promised by God.

Notes:_____

_____
_____
_____
_____
_____
_____
_____
_____
_____
_____
_____
_____
_____
_____
_____
_____
_____
_____
_____
_____

_____
_____
_____
_____
_____
_____
_____
_____
_____
_____
_____
_____
_____
_____
_____
_____
_____
_____
_____
_____
_____
_____
_____
_____
_____
_____
_____
_____
_____
_____
_____
_____
_____

Sunday, November 9

- Dedication of the Basilica of Saint John Lateran in Rome - Feast

First Reading: Ezekiel 47: 1-2, 8-9, 12
Responsorial Psalm: Psalms 46: 2-3, 5-6, 8-9
Second Reading: First Corinthians 3: 9c-11, 16-17
Alleluia: Second Chronicles 7: 16
Gospel: John 2: 13-22

Lectionary: 671

Every year on November 9th, the Catholic Church celebrates the Dedication of the Basilica of Saint John Lateran in Rome, also known as the Lateran Basilica. This cathedral church of Rome is the oldest and highest-ranking church in the Western world.

Today's readings resonate with the themes of dedication, God's presence, and the sacredness of the Church.

A Flowing River of Life (Ezekiel 47: 1-2, 8-9, 12):

1 And he brought me again to the gate of the house, and behold waters issued out from under the threshold of the house toward the east: for the forefront, of the house looked toward the east: but the waters came down to the right side of the temple to the south part of the altar.

2 And he led me out by the way of the north gate, and he caused me to turn to the way without the outward gate to the way that looked toward the east: and behold there ran out waters on the right side.

8 And he said to me: These waters that issue forth toward the hillocks of sand to the east, and go down to the plains of the desert, shall go into the sea, and shall go out, and the waters shall be healed.

9 And every living creature that creepeth whithersoever the torrent shall come, shall live: and there shall be fishes in abundance after these waters shall come thither, and they shall be healed, and all things shall live to which the torrent shall come.

12 And by the torrent on the banks thereof on both sides shall grow all trees that bear fruit: their leaf shall not fall off, and their fruit shall not fail: every month shall they bring forth firstfruits, because the waters thereof shall issue out of the sanctuary: and the fruits thereof shall be for food, and the leaves thereof for medicine.

The Book of Ezekiel opens the service with a beautiful symbolic image. The prophet describes a vision of water flowing from the Temple, bringing life and healing wherever it goes. This passage foreshadows the life-giving grace that flows from God and his Church.

Responsorial Psalm: Psalms 46: 2-3, 5-6, 8-9

R. (5) The waters of the river gladden the city of God, the holy dwelling of the Most High!

2 Our God is our refuge and strength: a helper in troubles, which have found us exceedingly.

3 Therefore we will not fear, when the earth shall be troubled; and the mountains shall be removed into the heart of the sea.

R. The waters of the river gladden the city of God, the holy dwelling of the Most High!

5 The stream of the river maketh the city of God joyful: the most High hath sanctified his own tabernacle.

6 God is in the midst thereof, it shall not be moved: God will help it in the morning early.

R. The waters of the river gladden the city of God, the holy dwelling of the Most High!

8 The Lord of armies is with us: the God of Jacob is our protector.

9 Come and behold ye the works of the Lord: what wonders he hath done upon earth,

R. The waters of the river gladden the city of God, the holy dwelling of the Most High!

Building on the Foundation (First Corinthians 3: 9c-11, 16-17):

9c You are God's husbandry; you are God's building.

10 According to the grace of God that is given to me, as a wise architect, I have laid the foundation; and another buildeth thereon. But let every man take heed how he buildeth thereupon.

11 For other foundation no man can lay, but that which is laid; which is Christ Jesus.

16 Know you not, that you are the temple of God, and that the Spirit of God dwelleth in you?

17 But if any man violate the temple of God, him shall God destroy. For the temple of God is holy, which you are.

The First Letter to Corinthians uses the metaphor of a building project to describe the Church. Paul reminds us that we are all co-workers with God, building a holy temple on the foundation of Jesus Christ. The passage emphasizes the importance of unity and right conduct within the Church.

Alleluia: Second Chronicles 7: 16

R. Alleluia, alleluia.

16 I have chosen and consecrated this house, says the Lord, that my name may be there forever.

R. Alleluia, alleluia.

Jesus Cleanses the Temple (John 2: 13-22):

13 And the pasch of the Jews was at hand, and Jesus went up to Jerusalem.

14 And he found in the temple them that sold oxen and sheep and doves, and the changers of money sitting.

15 And when he had made, as it were, a scourge of little cords, he drove them all out of the temple, the

sheep also and the oxen, and the money of the changers he poured out, and the tables he overthrew.

16 And to them that sold doves he said: Take these things hence, and make not the house of my Father a house of traffic.

17 And his disciples remembered, that it was written: The zeal of thy house hath eaten me up.

18 The Jews, therefore, answered, and said to him: What sign dost thou shew unto us, seeing thou dost these things?

19 Jesus answered, and said to them: Destroy this temple, and in three days I will raise it up.

20 The Jews then said: Six and forty years was this temple in building; and wilt thou raise it up in three days?

21 But he spoke of the temple of his body.

22 When therefore he was risen again from the dead, his disciples remembered, that he had said this, and they believed the scripture, and the word that Jesus had said.

The Gospel of John recounts the story of Jesus cleansing the Temple. His actions symbolize the importance of keeping the Church holy and dedicated to God's purposes. The passage also foreshadows Jesus' sacrifice, which would become the true temple where God dwells among his people.

Reflect and Respond:

- How can you contribute to building a strong and holy Church community?

- The first reading speaks of a flowing river of life. How can you share God's love and grace with others?

- The dedication of a church is a special occasion. If possible, consider visiting a church and spending some time in prayer or reflection.

A Prayer for Our Church:

Dear God, we thank you for the gift of your Church. May we, like the Basilica of Saint John Lateran, be a place of holiness, unity, and worship. Help us to be faithful stewards of your grace, building up your Church with love and dedication. Amen.

Living with Faith:

- This week, get involved in your church community. Attend a service, volunteer your time, or participate in a study group.

- Reflect on your own spiritual growth. Are there ways you can deepen your relationship with God?

- Be a beacon of God's love in the world. Show kindness and compassion to everyone you meet.

Notes:_____
_____
_____
_____
_____
_____
_____

Sunday, November 16

- Thirty-third Sunday in Ordinary Time

First Reading: Malachi 4: 1-2a

Responsorial Psalm: Psalms 98: 5-6, 7-8, 9

Second Reading: Second Thessalonians 3: 7-12

Alleluia: Luke 21: 28

Gospel: Luke 21: 5-19

Lectionary: 15

This Sunday's readings, while offering a glimpse of future judgement, ultimately point us towards hope and perseverance in the face of challenges. We encounter a call for justice, encouragement for diligence, and a reminder to stay focused on what truly matters.

The Day of the Lord (Malachi 4: 1-2a):

1 For behold the day shall come kindled as a furnace: and all the proud, and all that do wickedly shall be stubble: and the day that cometh shall set them on fire, saith the Lord of hosts, it shall not leave them root, nor branch.

2a But unto you that fear my name, the Sun of justice shall arise, and health in his wings.

The Book of Malachi opens the service with a message about the coming judgement day. The passage warns of the destruction of the wicked and the vindication of the righteous. This serves as a call to live a life of justice and integrity, prepared to meet God.

Responsorial Psalm: Psalms 98: 5-6, 7-8, 9

R. (9) The Lord comes to rule the earth with justice.

5 Sing praise to the Lord on the harp, on the harp, and with the voice of a psalm.

6 With long trumpets, and sound of comet. Make a joyful noise before the Lord our king.

R. The Lord comes to rule the earth with justice.

7 Let the sea be moved and the fulness thereof: the world and they that dwell therein.

8 The rivers shall clap their hands, the mountains shall rejoice together

R. The Lord comes to rule the earth with justice.

9 At the presence of the Lord: because he cometh to judge the earth. He shall judge the world with justice, and the people with equity.

R. The Lord comes to rule the earth with justice.

Work with Enthusiasm (Second Thessalonians 3: 7-12):

7 For yourselves know how you ought to imitate us: for we were not disorderly among you;

8 Neither did we eat any man's bread for nothing, but in labour and in toil we worked night and day, lest we should be chargeable to any of you.

9 Not as if we had not power: but that we might give ourselves a pattern unto you, to imitate us.

10 For also when we were with you, this we declared to you: that, if any man will not work, neither let him eat.

11 For we have heard there are some among you who walk disorderly, working not at all, but curiously meddling.

12 Now we charge them that are such, and beseech them by the Lord Jesus Christ, that, working with silence, they would eat their own bread.

The Second Letter to Thessalonians offers practical advice for Christian living. Paul encourages the Thessalonians to follow his example of hard work and to avoid idleness. The passage emphasizes the importance of living an orderly life and supporting those who are working for the Lord.

Alleluia: Luke 21: 28

R. Alleluia, alleluia.

28 Stand erect and raise your heads because your redemption is at hand.

R. Alleluia, alleluia.

Don't Be Deceived (Luke 21: 5-19):

5 And some saying of the temple, that it was adorned with goodly stones and gifts, he said:

6 These things which you see, the days will come in which there shall not be left a stone upon a stone that shall not be thrown down.

7 And they asked him, saying: Master, when shall these things be? and what shall be the sign when they shall begin to come to pass?

8 Who said: Take heed you be not seduced; for many will come in my name, saying, I am he; and the time is at hand: go ye not therefore after them.

9 And when you shall hear of wars and seditions, be not terrified: these things must first come to pass; but the end is not yet presently.

10 Then he said to them: Nation shall rise against nation, and kingdom against kingdom.

11 And there shall be great earthquakes in divers places, and pestilences, and famines, and terrors from heaven; and there shall be great signs.

12 But before all these things, they will lay their hands upon you, and persecute you, delivering you up to the synagogues and into prisons, dragging you before kings and governors, for my name's sake.

13 And it shall happen unto you for a testimony.

14 Lay it up therefore into your hearts, not to meditate before how you shall answer:

15 For I will give you a mouth and wisdom, which all your adversaries shall not be able to resist and gainsay.

16 And you shall be betrayed by your parents and brethren, and kinsmen and friends; and some of you they will put to death.

17 And you shall be hated by all men for my name's sake.

18 But a hair of your head shall not perish.

19 In your patience you shall possess your souls.

The Gospel of Luke presents Jesus' warnings about future troubles. He cautions his disciples not to be deceived by false prophets or discouraged by war, famine, and persecution. The passage reminds us to remain steadfast in our faith, knowing that God will be with us through all trials.

Reflect and Respond:

- How can you advocate for justice and fairness in your community?

- The reading from Thessalonians encourages us to work with enthusiasm. Are you diligent in your work and responsibilities?

- Jesus' warnings can be unsettling. How can you cultivate a sense of peace and hope in the midst of challenges?

A Prayer for Hope and Perseverance:

Dear God, grant us the courage to face challenges with faith and hope. Help us to distinguish truth from falsehood and to remain steadfast in our commitment to you. May we find strength in your word and encouragement in the fellowship of your Church. Amen.

Living with Faith:

- This week, research an organization working towards social justice in your community. Consider volunteering your time or donating to their cause.

- Identify one area of your life where you could be more diligent. Set a small, achievable goal and work towards it this week.

- Spend some time in prayer or meditation each day. Focus on finding peace and grounding yourself in God's presence.

Notes:_____
_____
_____
_____
_____
_____
_____
_____
_____
_____
_____
_____
_____

Sunday, November 23

- Christ the King - Solemnity

First Reading: Second Samuel 5: 1-3

Responsorial Psalm: Psalms 122: 1-2, 3-4ab, 4cd-5

Second Reading: Colossians 1: 12-20

Alleluia: Mark 11: 9, 10

Gospel: Luke 23: 35-43

Lectionary: 162

This Sunday, the final Sunday of the liturgical year, we celebrate the Solemnity of Our Lord Jesus Christ, King of the Universe, also referred to as Christ the King.

This feast day reminds us that Christ's reign extends over all creation, and that his kingship is one of love, service, and sacrifice.

David's Kingship Prepares for Christ's (Second Samuel 5: 1-3):

1 Then all the tribes of Israel came to David in Hebron, saying: Behold we are thy bone and thy flesh.

2 Moreover yesterday also and the day before, when Saul was king over us, thou wast he that did lead out and bring in Israel: and the Lord said to thee: Thou shalt feed my people Israel, and thou shalt be prince over Israel.

3 The ancients also of Israel came to the king to Hebron, and king David made a league with them in Hebron before the Lord: and they anointed David to be king over Israel.

The First Reading from the Second Book of Samuel recounts David's anointing as king over all Israel. David's reign foreshadows the eternal kingship of Christ, who is the true descendant of King David.

R. (1) Let us go rejoicing to the house of the Lord.

1 I rejoiced at the things that were said to me: We shall go into the house of the Lord.

2 Our feet were standing in thy courts, O Jerusalem.

R. Let us go rejoicing to the house of the Lord.

3 Jerusalem, which is built as a city, which is compact together.

4ab For thither did the tribes go up, the tribes of the Lord.

R. Let us go rejoicing to the house of the Lord.

4cd The testimony of Israel, to praise the name of the Lord.

5 Because their seats have sat in judgment, seats upon the house of David.

R. Let us go rejoicing to the house of the Lord.

Christ, the Universal King (Colossians 1: 12-20):

12 Giving thanks to God the Father, who hath made us worthy to be partakers of the lot of the saints in light:

13 Who hath delivered us from the power of darkness, and hath translated us into the kingdom of the Son of his love,

14 In whom we have redemption through his blood, the remission of sins;

15 Who is the image of the invisible God, the firstborn of every creature:

16 For in him were all things created in heaven and on earth, visible and invisible, whether thrones, or dominations, or principalities, or powers: all things were created by him and in him.

17 And he is before all, and by him all things consist.

18 And he is the head of the body, the church, who is the beginning, the firstborn from the dead; that in all things he may hold the primacy:

19 Because in him, it hath well pleased the Father, that all fullness should dwell;

20 And through him to reconcile all things unto himself, making peace through the blood of his cross, both as to the things that are on earth, and the things that are in heaven.

The Letter to the Colossians proclaims the majesty and dominion of Christ. The passage describes Christ as the firstborn of all creation, the image of the invisible God, and the one in whom all things hold together. This emphasizes the universality of Christ's reign, encompassing all creation.

Alleluia: Mark 11: 9, 10

R. Alleluia, alleluia.

9, 10 Blessed is he who comes in the name of the Lord! Blessed is the kingdom of our father David that is to come!

R. Alleluia, alleluia.

The King Who Serves (Luke 23: 35-43):

35 And the people stood beholding, and the rulers with them derided him, saying: He saved others; let him save himself, if he be Christ, the elect of God.

36 And the soldiers also mocked him, coming to him, and offering him vinegar,

37 And saying: If thou be the king of the Jews, save thyself.

38 And there was also a superscription written over him in letters of Greek, and Latin, and Hebrew: THIS IS THE KING OF THE JEWS.

39 And one of those robbers who were hanged, blasphemed him, saying: If thou be Christ, save thyself and us.

40 But the other answering, rebuked him, saying: Neither dost thou fear God, seeing thou art condemned under the same condemnation?

41 And we indeed justly, for we receive the due reward of our deeds; but this man hath done no evil.

42 And he said to Jesus: Lord, remember me when thou shalt come into thy kingdom.

43 And Jesus said to him: Amen I say to thee, this day thou shalt be with me in paradise.

The Gospel of Luke presents a powerful paradox. As Jesus hangs on the cross, mocked by the crowds and the rulers, an inscription proclaims him as "the King of the Jews." This image challenges our worldly understanding of kingship. Christ's reign is not one of earthly power, but of sacrificial love and service. The repentant thief crucified next to Jesus recognizes this truth and acknowledges Jesus' kingship.

Reflect and Respond:

- How does the image of Christ the King challenge your understanding of leadership and authority?

- The readings emphasize Christ's universal reign. How can you live your life in a way that acknowledges Christ's kingship in all areas?

- Consider the example of the repentant thief. Is there an area in your life where you need to acknowledge Jesus as your king?

A Prayer for a King Who Serves:

Dear God, we thank you for the gift of Jesus Christ, our King. May we follow his example of humility, service, and love. Help us to recognize your reign in all aspects of our lives, and to surrender our hearts to your loving kingship. Amen.

Living as Followers of the King:

- This week, look for opportunities to serve others. Volunteer your time to a cause you care about, or simply perform acts of kindness in your daily interactions.

- Reflect on your talents and gifts. Consider how you can

use them to glorify God and build his kingdom here on earth.

- Make Christ the King of your heart. Renew your commitment to following him and living according to his teachings.

Notes:_____

_____
_____
_____
_____
_____
_____
_____
_____
_____
_____
_____
_____
_____
_____
_____
_____
_____

_____
_____
_____
_____
_____
_____
_____
_____
_____
_____
_____
_____
_____
_____
_____
_____
_____
_____
_____
_____
_____
_____
_____

Sunday, November 30

- First Sunday of Advent

First Reading: Isaiah 2: 1-5

Responsorial Psalm: Psalms 122: 1-2, 3-4ab, 4cd-5, 6-7, 8-9

Second Reading: Romans 13: 11-14

Alleluia: Psalms 85: 8

Gospel: Matthew 24: 37-44

Lectionary: 1

The turning of the liturgical calendar brings us to the First Sunday of Advent, marking the beginning of a season of anticipation and preparation for the birth of Jesus Christ. Today's readings set the tone for this reflective period, urging us to cultivate hope, embrace a renewed way of living, and remain watchful for Christ's coming.

A Vision of Peace (Isaiah 2: 1-5):

1 The word that Isaias the son of Amos saw, concerning Juda and Jerusalem.

2 And in the last days the mountain of the house of the Lord shall be prepared on the top of mountains, and it shall be exalted above the hills, and all nations shall flow unto it.

3 And many people shall go, and say: Come and let us go up to the mountain of the Lord, and to the house of the God of Jacob, and he will teach us his ways, and we will walk in his paths: for the law shall come forth from Sion, and the word of the Lord from Jerusalem.

4 And he shall judge the Gentiles, and rebuke many people: and they shall turn their swords into ploughshares, and their spears into sickles: nation shall not lift up sword against nation, neither shall they be exercised any more to war.

5 O house of Jacob, come ye, and let us walk in the light of the Lord.

287

The Book of Isaiah opens the service with a message of hope. The prophet describes a future time when nations will turn away from war and violence, and instead walk in the light of the Lord. This passage establishes the hopeful spirit of Advent, a season of waiting for the Messiah who will bring peace and salvation to the world.

Responsorial Psalm: Psalms 122: 1-2, 3-4ab, 4cd-5, 6-7, 8-9

R. (1) Let us go rejoicing to the house of the Lord.

1 I rejoiced at the things that were said to me: We shall go into the house of the Lord.

2 Our feet were standing in thy courts, O Jerusalem.

R. Let us go rejoicing to the house of the Lord.

3 Jerusalem, which is built as a city, which is compact together.

4ab For thither did the tribes go up, the tribes of the Lord.

R. Let us go rejoicing to the house of the Lord.

4cd The testimony of Israel, to praise the name of the Lord.

5 Because their seats have sat in judgment, seats upon the house of David.

R. Let us go rejoicing to the house of the Lord.

6 Pray ye for the things that are for the peace of Jerusalem: and abundance for them that love thee.

7 Let peace be in thy strength: and abundance in thy towers.

R. Let us go rejoicing to the house of the Lord.

8 For the sake of my brethren, and of my neighbours, I spoke peace of thee.

9 Because of the house of the Lord our God, I have sought good things for thee.

R. Let us go rejoicing to the house of the Lord.

Waking Up to Christ's Arrival (Romans 13: 11-14):

11 And that knowing the season; that it is now the hour for us to rise from sleep. For now our salvation is nearer than when we believed.

12 The night is passed, and the day is at hand. Let us therefore cast off the works of darkness, and put on the armour of light.

13 Let us walk honestly, as in the day: not in rioting and drunkenness, not in chambering and impurities, not in contention and envy:

14 But put ye on the Lord Jesus Christ, and make not provision for the flesh in its concupiscences.

The Letter to the Romans reminds us that salvation is drawing near and calls us to live according to Christ's teachings. The passage uses the metaphor of putting on the armor of light, symbolizing a commitment to living a good and holy life. It emphasizes casting aside sinful behavior and living in a way that prepares us for the coming of Christ.

Alleluia: Psalms 85: 8

R. Alleluia, alleluia.

8 Show us Lord, your love; and grant us your salvation.

R. Alleluia, alleluia.

Be Ready, for the Son of Man is Coming (Matthew 24: 37-44):

37 And as in the days of Noe, so shall also the coming of the Son of man be.

38 For as in the days before the flood, they were eating and drinking, marrying and giving in marriage, even till that day in which Noe entered into the ark,

39 And they knew not till the flood came, and took them all away; so also shall the coming of the Son of man be.

40 Then two shall be in the field: one shall be taken, and one shall be left.

41 Two women shall be grinding at the mill: one shall be taken, and one shall be left.

42 Watch ye therefore, because ye know not what hour your Lord will come.

43 But know this ye, that if the goodman of the house knew at what hour the thief would come, he would certainly watch, and would not suffer his house to be broken open.

44 Wherefore be you also ready, because at what hour you know not the Son of man will come.

The Gospel of Matthew presents a parable about the importance of being watchful and prepared for the second coming of Christ. Jesus compares his coming to a thief at night. No one knows the exact hour, so we must be vigilant at all times. This parable serves as a call to action throughout the Advent season, urging us to remain alert and committed to our faith.

Reflecting on the Season:

- How can you cultivate a sense of hope and anticipation during Advent?

- The reading from Romans talks about putting on the armor of light. What steps can you take to live a more Christ-centered life?

- The parable emphasizes the importance of being prepared. How can you prepare your heart and mind for the celebration of Jesus' birth?

Living with Hope and Readiness:

- Dedicate time to prayer and reflection during Advent. Consider meditating on scripture or journaling about your thoughts and feelings.

- Set some personal Advent goals. This could involve acts of charity, increased prayer time, or focusing on reading scripture.

- Light an Advent wreath. This beautiful tradition

visually represents the progress of the Advent season. Each week, a new candle is lit, symbolizing the growing light of hope as Christmas approaches.

- Minimize distractions and focus on what truly matters. Advent is a time to simplify your life and strengthen your relationship with God.

Prayer

Gracious God,

As Advent begins, fill us with hope, like Isaiah's vision of peace. We yearn for Your light, ready to shed darkness and live according to Your teachings.

Make us watchful, like the servants in Matthew's parable. Guide our steps in preparation for Christ's coming.

Bless our Advent journey with light, reflection, and a deepening relationship with You. Amen.

Notes:_____
_____
_____
_____
_____
_____
_____
_____
_____
_____
_____
_____
_____
_____
_____
_____
_____
_____
_____
_____
_____
_____
_____
_____
_____
_____
_____

December 2025

Sunday, December 7

- Second Sunday of Advent

First Reading: Isaiah 11: 1-10

Responsorial Psalm: Psalms 72: 1-2, 7-8, 12-13, 17

Second Reading: Romans 15: 4-9

Alleluia: Luke 3: 4, 6

Gospel: Matthew 3: 1-12

Lectionary: 4

The Second Sunday of Advent finds us further along the liturgical journey towards Christmas. Today's readings focus on themes of preparation, the promise of a renewed world, and the voice crying out in the wilderness – John the Baptist.

A Branch from Jesse (Isaiah 11: 1-10):

1 And there shall come forth a rod out of the root of Jesse, and a flower shall rise up out of his root.

2 And the spirit of the Lord shall rest upon him: the spirit of wisdom, and of understanding, the spirit of counsel, and of fortitude, the spirit of knowledge, and of godliness.

3 And he shall be filled with the spirit of the fear of the Lord. He shall not judge according to the sight of the eyes, nor reprove according to the hearing of the ears.

4 But he shall judge the poor with justice, and shall reprove with equity for the meek of the earth: land he shall strike the earth with the rod of his mouth, and with the breath of his lips he shall slay the wicked.

5 And justice shall be the girdle of his loins: and faith the girdle of his reins.

6 The wolf shall dwell with the lamb: and the leopard shall lie down with the kid: the calf and the lion, and the sheep shall abide together, and a little child shall lead them.

7 The calf and the bear shall feed: their young ones shall rest together: and the lion shall eat straw like the ox.

8 And the sucking child shall play on the hole of the asp: and the weaned child shall thrust his hand into the den of the basilisk.

9 They shall not hurt, nor shall they kill in all my holy mountain, for the earth is filled with the knowledge of the Lord, as the covering waters of the sea.

10 In that day the root of Jesse, who standeth for an ensign of the people, him the Gentiles shall beseech, and his sepulchre shall be glorious.

The Book of Isaiah opens the service with a beautiful prophecy. The passage describes a shoot that will grow from the stump of Jesse, the father of King David. This shoot symbolizes the coming Messiah, who will usher in an era of peace and justice. The prophet paints a picture of a world where harmony prevails between all creation, including humans and animals. This passage kindles hope for a future transformed by God's grace.

Responsorial Psalm: Psalms 72: 1-2, 7-8, 12-13, 17

R. (7) Justice shall flourish in his time, and fullness of peace for ever.

1-2 Give to the king thy judgment, O God: and to the king's son thy justice: To judge thy people with justice, and thy poor with judgment.

R. Justice shall flourish in his time, and fullness of peace for ever.

7 In his days shall justice spring up, and abundance of peace, till the moon be taken sway.

8 And he shall rule from sea to sea, and from the river unto the ends of the earth.

R. Justice shall flourish in his time, and fullness of peace for ever.

12 For he shall deliver the poor from the mighty: and the needy that had no helper.

13 He shall spare the poor and needy: and he shall save the souls of the poor.

R. Justice shall flourish in his time, and fullness of peace for ever.

17 Let his name be blessed for evermore: his name continueth before the sun. And in him shall all the tribes of the earth be blessed: all nations shall magnify him.

R. Justice shall flourish in his time, and fullness of peace for ever.

Living in Harmony (Romans 15: 4-9):

4 For what things soever were written, were written for our learning: that through patience and the comfort of the scriptures, we might have hope.

5 Now the God of patience and of comfort grant you to be of one mind one towards another, according to Jesus Christ:

6 That with one mind, and with one mouth, you may glorify God and the Father of our Lord Jesus Christ.

7 Wherefore receive one another, as Christ also hath received you unto the honour of God.

8 For I say that Christ Jesus was minister of the circumcision for the truth of God, to confirm the promises made unto the fathers.

9 But that the Gentiles are to glorify God for his mercy, as it is written: Therefore will I confess to thee, O Lord, among the Gentiles, and will sing to thy name.

The Letter to the Romans emphasizes the importance of unity and mutual encouragement within the Christian community. The passage reminds us to find joy in the hope that we share and to live in such a way that builds one another up. This fosters a spirit of peace and love, reflecting the message of Isaiah's prophecy.

Alleluia: Luke 3: 4, 6

R. Alleluia, alleluia.

4, 6 Prepare the way of the Lord, make straight his paths: all flesh shall see the salvation of God.

R. Alleluia, alleluia.

Prepare the Way of the Lord (Matthew 3: 1-12):

1 And in those days cometh John the Baptist preaching in the desert of Judea.

2 And saying: Do penance: for the kingdom of heaven is at hand.

3 For this is he that was spoken of by Isaias the prophet, saying: A voice of one crying in the desert, Prepare ye the way of the Lord, make straight his paths.

4 And the same John had his garment of camels' hair, and a leathern girdle about his loins: and his meat was locusts and wild honey.

5 Then went out to him Jerusalem and all Judea, and all the country about Jordan:

6 And were baptized by him in the Jordan, confessing their sins.

7 And seeing many of the Pharisees and Sadducees coming to his baptism, he said to them: Ye brood of vipers, who hath shewed you to flee from the wrath to come?

8 Bring forth therefore fruit worthy of penance.

9 And think not to say within yourselves, We have Abraham for our father. For I tell you that God is able of these stones to raise up children to Abraham.

10 For now the axe is laid to the root of the trees. Every tree therefore that doth not yield good fruit, shall be cut down, and cast into the fire.

11 I indeed baptize you in the water unto penance, but he that shall come after me, is mightier than I, whose shoes I am not worthy to bear; he shall baptize you in the Holy Ghost and fire.

12 Whose fan is in his hand, and he will thoroughly cleanse his floor and gather his wheat into the barn; but the chaff he will burn with unquenchable fire.

The Gospel of Matthew introduces John the Baptist, a pivotal figure who prepares the way for Jesus' coming. John appears in the wilderness, preaching a message of repentance and calling on the people to prepare for the coming of the Lord. The passage emphasizes the importance of making a change of heart and living a life that reflects God's will.

Reflecting on Preparation:

- How can you contribute to building a more peaceful and harmonious world?

- The reading from Romans talks about living in a way that builds others up. Consider someone in your life who could benefit from your encouragement. Reach out to them and offer words of support.

- John the Baptist's message is a call to repentance. Is there an area in your life where you need to make a change?

Prayer

Dear God, as we journey through this Advent season, guide us on the path of preparation. Help us to make room in our hearts for the coming of Christ. Grant us the courage to turn away from sin and embrace a life that reflects your will. May we find joy in the hope of your promise and work towards building a more peaceful and harmonious world. We pray in Jesus' name. Amen.

Living with Purpose:

- This week, consider volunteering your time or resources to a cause that promotes peace and justice.

- Reflect on your relationships with others. Are there ways you can strengthen these connections and build a more supportive community?

- Make a conscious effort to live a life that reflects God's values. This could involve acts of service, kindness, and compassion towards others.

Notes:_____

_____

_____

_____

_____

_____

_____

_____

_____

_____

_____

_____

_____

_____

_____

_____

_____

_____

_____

_____

_____

_____

_____

Sunday, December 14

- Third Sunday of Advent

First Reading: Isaiah 35: 1-6a, 10

Responsorial Psalm: Psalms 146: 6-7, 8-9a, 9bc-10

Second Reading: James 5: 7-10

Alleluia: Isaiah 61: 1

Gospel: Matthew 11: 2-11

Lectionary: 7

This Sunday, known as Gaudete Sunday (Latin for "Rejoice"), marks the midpoint of the Advent season. Today's readings offer a message of hope, perseverance, and the joyful anticipation of Christ's arrival.

The Wilderness Shall Bloom (Isaiah 35: 1-6a, 10):

1 The land that was desolate and impassable shall be glad, and the wilderness shall rejoice, and shall flourish like the lily.

2 It shall bud forth and blossom, and shall rejoice with joy and praise: the glory of Libanus is given to it: the beauty of Carmel, and Saron, they shall see the glory of the Lord, and the beauty of our God.

3 Strengthen ye the feeble hands, and confirm the weak knees.

4 Say to the fainthearted: Take courage, and fear not: behold your God will bring the revenge of recompense: God himself will come and will save you.

5 Then shall the eyes of the blind be opened, and the ears of the deaf shall be unstopped.

6a Then shall the lame man leap as a hart, and the tongue of the dumb shall be free.

10 And the redeemed of the Lord shall return, and shall come into Sion with praise, and everlasting joy shall be upon their heads: they shall obtain joy and gladness, and sorrow and mourning shall flee away.

The Book of Isaiah opens the service with a vibrant image of transformation. The prophet describes a barren wilderness blossoming into a fruitful land. This passage symbolizes the joy and restoration that Christ will bring to the world. It reminds us that even in the midst of hardship, God's love can bring forth beauty and hope.

Responsorial Psalm: Psalms 146: 6-7, 8-9a, 9bc-10

R. (Is 35:4) Lord, come and save us.

Or R. Alleluia.

6 The LORD God made heaven and earth, the sea, and all things that are in them.

7 The LORD God keepeth truth for ever: who executeth judgment for them that suffer wrong: who giveth food to the hungry. The Lord looseth them that are fettered:

R. Lord, come and save us.

Or R. Alleluia.

8 The Lord enlighteneth the blind. The Lord lifteth up them that are cast down: the Lord loveth the just.

9a The Lord keepeth the strangers.

R. Lord, come and save us.

Or R. Alleluia.

9bc He will support the fatherless and the widow: and the ways of sinners he will destroy.

10 The Lord shall reign for ever: thy God, O Sion, unto generation and generation.

R. Lord, come and save us.

Or R. Alleluia.

Be Patient, for the Lord's Coming is Near (James 5: 7-10):

7 Be patient therefore, brethren, until the coming of the Lord. Behold, the husbandman waiteth for the precious fruit of the earth:

patiently bearing till he receive the early and latter rain.

8 Be you therefore also patient, and strengthen your hearts: for the coming of the Lord is at hand.

9 Grudge not, brethren, one against another, that you may not be judged. Behold the judge standeth before the door.

10 Take, my brethren, for an example of suffering evil, of labour and patience, the prophets, who spoke in the name of the Lord.

The Letter of James encourages patience and perseverance as we wait for the coming of the Lord. The passage reminds us to be like farmers who wait patiently for their crops to grow. Just as they wait with hope, we are called to wait with faith and trust in God's timing.

Alleluia: Isaiah 61: 1

R. Alleluia, alleluia.

1 The Spirit of the Lord is upon me, because he has anointed me to bring glad tidings to the poor.

R. Alleluia, alleluia.

Are You the One Who is to Come? (Matthew 11: 2-11):

2 Now when John had heard in prison the works of Christ: sending two of his disciples he said to him:

3 Art thou he that art to come, or look we for another?

4 And Jesus making answer said to them: Go and relate to John what you have heard and seen.

5 The blind see, the lame walk, the lepers are cleansed, the deaf hear, the dead rise again, the poor have the gospel preached to them.

6 And blessed is he that shall not be scandalized in me.

7 And when they went their way, Jesus began to say to the multitudes concerning John: What went you out into the desert to see? a reed shaken with the wind?

8 But what went you out to see? a man clothed in soft garments? Behold they that are clothed in soft garments, are in the houses of kings.

9 But what went you out to see? a prophet? yea I tell you, and more than a prophet.

10 For this is he of whom it is written: Behold I send my angel before thy face, who shall prepare thy way before thee.

11 Amen I say to you, there hath not risen among them that are born of women a greater than John the Baptist: yet he that is the lesser in the kingdom of heaven is greater than he.

The Gospel of Matthew presents a poignant exchange between John the Baptist and Jesus. John, imprisoned and questioning, sends disciples to Jesus to ask if he is the Messiah. Jesus responds by pointing to his works – healing the sick, raising the dead, and proclaiming good news to the poor. This passage affirms Jesus' identity as the fulfillment of prophecy and the source of hope for the world.

Reflecting on Hope and Joy:

- How can you cultivate a sense of joy and anticipation during the remaining weeks of Advent?

- The reading from James talks about patience. Is there an area in your life where you need to practice more patience?

- Jesus' works highlight his compassion and love. How can you reflect these qualities in your own life?

Living with Anticipation:

- Spend time this week reflecting on the blessings in your life, big and small. Gratitude fosters joy.

- Reach out to someone who might be feeling alone or discouraged. Offer them a listening ear and words of encouragement.

- Consider acts of charity or service that bring hope and joy to others in your community.

A Prayer for Hope and Joy:

Dear God, fill our hearts with the joy of the approaching celebration of your Son's birth. Grant us patience as we await his coming and the fulfillment of your promises. May we see the signs of hope and transformation in the world around us, and live in joyful anticipation of the light that Christ brings. Amen.

Notes:_____

_____

_____

_____

_____

_____

_____

_____

_____

_____

_____

_____

_____

Sunday, December 21

- Fourth Sunday of Advent

First Reading: Isaiah 7: 10-14

Responsorial Psalm: Psalms 24: 1-2, 3-4, 5-6

Second Reading: Romans 1: 1-7

Alleluia: Matthew 1: 23

Gospel: Matthew 1: 18-24

Lectionary: 10

This Sunday, the Fourth Sunday of Advent, marks the final week before Christmas. Today's readings focus on the fulfillment of God's promises, the faithfulness of God, and the miraculous conception of Jesus Christ.

A Sign is Given (Isaiah 7: 10-14):

10 And the Lord spoke again to Achaz, saying:

11 Ask thee a sign of the Lord thy God either unto the depth of hell, or unto the height above.

12 And Achaz said: I will not ask, and I will not tempt the Lord.

13 And he said: Hear ye therefore, O house of David: Is it a small thing for you to be grievous to men, that you are grievous to my God also?

14 Therefore the Lord himself shall give you a sign. Behold a virgin shall conceive, and bear a son, and his name shall be called Emmanuel.

The Book of Isaiah opens the service with a powerful message. In the midst of political turmoil, God promises a sign to King Ahaz: a virgin will conceive and bear a son. This son, Immanuel, which means "God is with us," foreshadows the coming of Jesus Christ, the fulfillment of God's promise to send a savior.

Responsorial Psalm: Psalms 24: 1-2, 3-4, 5-6

R. (7c and 10b) Let the Lord enter; he is king of glory.

1 The earth is the Lord's and the fulness thereof: the world, and all they that dwell therein.

2 For he hath founded it upon the seas; and hath prepared it upon the rivers.

R. Let the Lord enter; he is king of glory.

3 Who shall ascend into the mountain of the Lord: or who shall stand in his holy place?

4 The innocent in hands, and clean of heart, who hath not taken his soul in vain, nor sworn deceitfully to his neighbour.

R. Let the Lord enter; he is king of glory.

5 He shall receive a blessing from the Lord, and mercy from God his Saviour.

6 This is the generation of them that seek him, of them that seek the face of the God of Jacob.

R. Let the Lord enter; he is king of glory.

God's Faithfulness (Romans 1: 1-7):

1 Paul, a servant of Jesus Christ, called to be an apostle, separated unto the gospel of God,

2 Which he had promised before, by his prophets, in the holy scriptures,

3 Concerning his Son, who was made to him of the seed of David, according to the flesh,

4 Who was predestinated the Son of God in power, according to the spirit of sanctification, by the resurrection of our Lord Jesus Christ from the dead;

5 By whom we have received grace and apostleship for obedience to the faith, in all nations, for his name;

6 Among whom are you also the called of Jesus Christ:

7 To all that are at Rome, the beloved of God, called to be saints. Grace to you, and peace from God our Father, and from the Lord Jesus Christ.

The Letter to the Romans emphasizes God's faithfulness in keeping his promises. The passage speaks of the gospel, the good news of Jesus Christ, which has been promised beforehand through the prophets. This reinforces the message of Isaiah's prophecy and highlights the long-awaited arrival of the Messiah.

Alleluia: Matthew 1: 23

R. Alleluia, alleluia.

23 The virgin shall conceive, and bear a son, and they shall name him Emmanuel.

R. Alleluia, alleluia.

The Birth of Jesus (Matthew 1: 18-24):

18 Now the generation of Christ was in this wise. When as his mother Mary was espoused to Joseph, before they came together, she was found with child, of the Holy Ghost.

19 Whereupon Joseph her husband, being a just man, and not willing publicly to expose her, was minded to put her away privately.

20 But while he thought on these things, behold the angel of the Lord appeared to him in his sleep, saying: Joseph, son of David, fear not to take unto thee Mary thy wife, for that which is conceived in her, is of the Holy Ghost.

21 And she shall bring forth a son: and thou shalt call his name JESUS. For he shall save his people from their sins.

22 Now all this was done that it might be fulfilled which the Lord spoke by the prophet, saying:

23 Behold a virgin shall be with child, and bring forth a son, and they shall call his name Emmanuel, which being interpreted is, God with us.

24 And Joseph rising up from sleep, did as the angel of the Lord had

The Gospel of Matthew presents the story of the angel Gabriel appearing to Joseph and announcing the miraculous conception of Jesus in Mary's womb. Joseph, a righteous man, is instructed to take Mary as his wife and to name the child Jesus. This passage marks the pivotal moment when the promise of God takes human form.

Reflecting on the Promise:

- How does the concept of Immanuel, "God is with us," bring you comfort and hope?

- The readings emphasize God's faithfulness. Reflect on a time in your life when you experienced God's faithfulness in keeping a promise.

- The birth of Jesus signifies a new beginning. Is there an area in your life where you are hoping for a fresh start?

Living with Anticipation:

- This week, focus on acts of kindness and generosity towards others, reflecting the spirit of the coming celebration.

- Spend time in prayer or reflection, preparing your heart for the birth of Christ.

- Consider attending a Christmas Eve service or participating in another tradition that celebrates the arrival of Jesus.

A Prayer of Anticipation:

Dear God, as we stand on the threshold of celebrating the birth of your Son, we thank you for your faithfulness in fulfilling your promises. May the coming of Christ fill our hearts with joy, hope, and peace. Help us to prepare our hearts for his arrival and to embrace the new beginnings he offers. Amen.

Notes:_____

_____
_____
_____
_____
_____
_____
_____
_____
_____
_____
_____
_____
_____
_____
_____
_____
_____
_____
_____
_____
_____
_____
_____
_____
_____
_____
_____
_____
_____
_____

Sunday, December 28

- The Holy Family - Feast

First Reading: Sirach 3: 2-6, 12-14

Responsorial Psalm: Psalms 128: 1-2, 3, 4-5

Second Reading: Colossians 3: 12-21 or Colossians 3: 12-17

Alleluia: Colossians 3: 15a, 16a

Gospel: Matthew 2: 13-15, 19-23

Lectionary: 17

The Sunday after Christmas is designated as the Feast of the Holy Family, honoring Jesus, Mary, and Joseph as a model for Christian families. Today's readings highlight the importance of family life, the virtues present within the Holy Family, and the challenges they faced.

The Importance of Family (Sirach 3: 2-6, 12-14):

2 For God hath made the father honourable to the children: and seeking the judgment of the mothers, hath confirmed it upon the children.

3 He that loveth God, shall obtain pardon for his sins by prayer, and shall refrain himself from them, and shall be heard in the prayer of days.

4 And he that honoureth his mother is as one that layeth up a treasure.

5 He that honoureth his father shall have joy in his own children, and in the day of his prayer he shall be heard.

6 He that honoureth his father shall enjoy a long life: and he that obeyeth the father, shall be a comfort to his mother.

12 Son, support the old age of thy father, and grieve him not in his life;

13 And if his understanding fail, have patience with him, and despise

him not when thou art in thy strength: for the relieving of the father shall not be forgotten.

14 For good shall be repaid to thee for the sin of thy mother.

The Book of Sirach opens the service with a message about honoring one's parents. The passage emphasizes the importance of respecting and caring for our families. This sets the stage for understanding the Holy Family as an example of love, respect, and obedience within the family unit.

Responsorial Psalm: Psalms 128: 1-2, 3, 4-5

R. (1) Blessed are those who fear the Lord and walk in his ways.

1 Blessed are all they that fear the Lord: that walk in his ways.

2 For thou shalt eat the labours of thy hands: blessed art thou, and it shall be well with thee.

R. Blessed are those who fear the Lord and walk in his ways.

3 Thy wife as a fruitful vine, on the sides of thy house.

R. Blessed are those who fear the Lord and walk in his ways.

4 Behold, thus shall the man be blessed that feareth the Lord.

5 May the Lord bless thee out of Sion: and mayest thou see the good things of Jerusalem all the days of thy life.

R. Blessed are those who fear the Lord and walk in his ways.

Putting on Christ (Colossians 3: 12-21 or Colossians 3: 12-17):

12 Put ye on therefore, as the elect of God, holy, and beloved, the bowels of mercy, benignity, humility, modesty, patience:

13 Bearing with one another, and forgiving one another, if any have a complaint against another: even as the Lord hath forgiven you, so do you also.

14 But above all these things have charity, which is the bond of perfection:

15 And let the peace of Christ rejoice in your hearts, wherein also you are called in one body: and be ye thankful.

16 Let the word of Christ dwell in you abundantly, in all wisdom: teaching and admonishing one another in psalms, hymns, and spiritual canticles, singing in grace in your hearts to God.

17 All whatsoever you do in word or in work, do all in the name of the Lord Jesus Christ, giving thanks to God and the Father by him.

18 Wives, be subject to your husbands, as it behoveth in the Lord.

19 Husbands, love your wives, and be not bitter towards them.

20 Children, obey your parents in all things: for this is well pleasing to the Lord.

21 Fathers, provoke not your children to indignation, lest they be discouraged.

Or

12 Put ye on therefore, as the elect of God, holy, and beloved, the bowels of mercy, benignity, humility, modesty, patience:

13 Bearing with one another, and forgiving one another, if any have a complaint against another: even as the Lord hath forgiven you, so do you also.

14 But above all these things have charity, which is the bond of perfection:

15 And let the peace of Christ rejoice in your hearts, wherein also you are called in one body: and be ye thankful.

16 Let the word of Christ dwell in you abundantly, in all wisdom: teaching and admonishing one another in psalms, hymns, and spiritual canticles, singing in grace in your hearts to God.

17 All whatsoever you do in word or in work, do all in the name of the Lord Jesus Christ, giving thanks to God and the Father by him.

The Letter to the Colossians provides guidance for Christian living. The passage encourages us to cultivate virtues such as compassion, kindness, humility, gentleness, and patience – qualities evident within the Holy Family. This reminds us to strive to embody these same virtues in our own relationships.

R. Alleluia, alleluia.

15a, 16a Let the peace of Christ control your hearts; let the word of Christ dwell in you richly.

R. Alleluia, alleluia.

Flight and Return (Matthew 2: 13-15, 19-23):

13 And after they were departed, behold an angel of the Lord appeared in sleep to Joseph, saying: Arise, and take the child and his mother, and fly into Egypt: and be there until I shall tell thee. For it will come to pass that Herod will seek the child to destroy him.

14 Who arose, and took the child and his mother by night, and retired into Egypt: and he was there until the death of Herod:

15 That it might be fulfilled which the Lord spoke by the prophet, saying: Out of Egypt have I called my son.

19 But when Herod was dead, behold an angel of the Lord appeared in sleep to Joseph in Egypt,

20 Saying: Arise, and take the child and his mother, and go into the land of Israel. For they are dead that sought the life of the child.

21 Who arose, and took the child and his mother, and came into the land of Israel.

22 But hearing that Archelaus reigned in Judea in the room of Herod his father, he was afraid to go thither: and being warned in sleep retired into the quarters of Galilee.

23 And coming he dwelt in a city called Nazareth: that it might be fulfilled which was said by prophets: That he shall be called a Nazarene.

The Gospel of Matthew recounts the Holy Family's flight to Egypt to escape King Herod's murderous decree. After Herod's death, they are instructed by an angel to return to their homeland. This passage highlights the challenges and dangers faced by the Holy Family, demonstrating their resilience and faith in God's protection.

Reflecting on the Holy Family:

- How can you strengthen the bonds within your own family?

- The reading from Colossians mentions virtues like kindness and compassion. Consider ways to incorporate these qualities more fully into your family interactions.

- The Holy Family faced adversity but persevered through faith. Is there a challenge you are facing within your family that you can approach with faith and trust in God?

Living as a Family:

- Plan a special family activity or meal this week to celebrate the importance of family togetherness.
- Discuss the roles of each member of the Holy Family and how they can inspire your own family dynamic.
- Pray together as a family, asking for God's blessings and guidance.

A Prayer for Families:

Dear God, we thank you for the gift of the Holy Family, a model of love, faith, and perseverance. Bless our families with your love and grace. May we learn from the example of the Holy Family and strive to create a loving and supportive environment within our own homes. Guide us in times of difficulty and help us to grow closer to one another and to you. Amen.

Notes:_____
_____
_____
_____

_____
_____
_____
_____

Conclusion: A Year of Grace, A Lifetime of Faith

As we close the *2025 Roman Catholic Sunday Missal*, let us take a moment to reflect on the profound journey we have undertaken together. Week by week, Sunday by Sunday, this book has been a companion, guiding you through the rhythms of the liturgical year, immersing you in the sacred mysteries of our faith, and inviting you to encounter the living Christ in Word and Sacrament.

A Year of Encounter

Each Sunday, you heard God's voice in Scripture, offering wisdom, comfort, and challenge. You joined your parish family in worship, lifting your heart in prayer and praise. You approached the Eucharistic table, receiving the Body and Blood of Christ, the bread of heaven that sustains us on our journey of faith.

This year has been a time of grace—grace that strengthened you in times of trial, inspired you in moments of joy, and called you ever deeper into relationship with the God who loves you beyond measure.

The Lessons We Carry

The liturgical year has taught us much:

- **In Advent**, we learned the beauty of waiting with hope and preparing our hearts for the coming of Christ.

- **At Christmas**, we celebrated the wonder of God becoming man, the infinite taking on the finite, to dwell among us.

- **Through Ordinary Time**, we walked alongside Jesus, listening to His teachings, witnessing His miracles, and learning how to follow Him in our daily lives.

- **In Lent**, we entered the desert, embracing sacrifice and penance as we journeyed toward the cross.

- **At Easter**, we rejoiced in the victory of life over death, light over darkness, and love over sin.

- **In the solemnities and feasts**, we honored the saints, celebrated Mary as the Mother of God, and deepened our understanding of the mysteries of our faith.

Every season, every celebration, every reading has left its imprint on our hearts, shaping us into disciples who are better equipped to carry Christ's light into the world.

A Call to Continue

Although this liturgical year has come to an end, the journey of faith never ends. As Catholics, we are called to live out the truths we have learned, to make every day a reflection of the love and mercy we have encountered in Christ.

This missal has been a guide for your Sundays, but its lessons are meant to inspire your daily life. Carry the wisdom of the Scriptures into your conversations, decisions, and actions. Let the prayers you've prayed deepen your intimacy with God. Let the challenges you've embraced motivate you to serve others with compassion and humility.

Strengthened by Community

The journey of faith is not one we walk alone. Throughout this year, you have been part of a global community of believers, united by one faith, one baptism, and one Lord. Together, we have worshipped, prayed, and grown in grace.

As you continue to participate in the life of the Church, remember the strength that comes from belonging to this universal family. Lean on your parish community, support one another in times of need, and celebrate the joys and milestones of faith together.

Living the Eucharistic Life

The Eucharist, the source and summit of our faith, is not confined to the walls of the church. It is a call to live as Christ lived—to give of ourselves in love, to be bread broken for others, and to be vessels of God's grace in the world.

As you move forward, let the Eucharist be the center of your life. Let its transformative power shape your thoughts, words, and deeds, so that you may truly become what you receive: the Body of Christ, alive and active in the world.

Looking Ahead

As we turn the page to a new liturgical year, let us carry the light of this journey with us. There will be new challenges to face, new joys to celebrate, and new opportunities to grow in faith. Trust that God, who has been faithful throughout this year, will continue to guide and sustain you.

"I am with you always, until the end of the age." (Matthew 28:20)

This promise of Christ is our assurance and our hope. Wherever life takes you, whatever trials you encounter, know that you are never alone. God walks with you, His Spirit empowers you, and His Church supports you.

A Final Prayer

Let us end this journey with a prayer of thanksgiving:

Heavenly Father, we thank You for the gift of this year, for the grace to walk through its seasons and for the wisdom gained along the way. Thank You for Your Word, which has guided us, and for the Eucharist, which has nourished us. As we move forward, may we carry the light of Christ into every corner of our lives, living as witnesses to Your love and mercy. Strengthen us to face the challenges ahead with faith, hope, and love, and bring us one day into the fullness of Your kingdom. We ask this through Christ our Lord. Amen.

Until We Meet Again

May this missal continue to serve as a source of inspiration and strength. As you close its pages, know that the story of God's love is still unfolding in your life. Go forth with joy, knowing that you are deeply loved and called to share that love with the world.

"May the Lord bless you and keep you; may the Lord make His face shine upon you and be gracious to you; may the Lord lift up His countenance upon you and give you peace." (Numbers 6:24-26)

Thank you for allowing this book to be part of your spiritual journey. Until we meet again in another liturgical year, may the peace of Christ reign in your heart.

Made in the USA
Las Vegas, NV
26 June 2025